"Although Handel's *Messiah* is known and loved by many, the composer's intentions and purpose in creating this unique work are either unknown or underappreciated. . . . In this book Calvin Stapert's aim is not merely to give his readers information about this remarkable oratorio; he wants them to *understand* it — an aim admirably achieved with clarity, conviction, and charm."

— ROBIN A. LEAVER
Yale Institute of Sacred Music
Queen's University Belfast

"A superb general treatment of a cornerstone in Western cultural history, Stapert's book is a work of great intelligence and devotional warmth. Highly recommended."

— STEPHEN A. CRIST
Emory University

Handel's *Messiah*

Comfort for God's People

Calvin R. Stapert

WILLIAM B. EERDMANS PUBLISHING COMPANY

GRAND RAPIDS, MICHIGAN / CAMBRIDGE, U.K.

Published 2010 by
Wm. B. Eerdmans Publishing Co.
2140 Oak Industrial Drive N.E., Grand Rapids, Michigan 49505 /
P.O. Box 163, Cambridge CB3 9PU U.K.

Printed in the United States of America

16 15 14 13 12 11 10   7 6 5 4 3 2 1

Library of Congress Cataloging-in-Publication Data

Stapert, Calvin, 1942-
Handel's Messiah: comfort for God's people / Calvin R. Stapert.
p.   cm. — (Calvin Institute of Christian Worship liturgical studies series)
Includes bibliographical references and index.
ISBN 978-0-8028-6587-8 (pbk.: alk. paper)
1. Handel, George Frideric, 1685-1759. Messiah.   I. Title.

ML410.H13S66   2010

782.23 — dc22

2010036375

www.eerdmans.com

To the Calvin Oratorio Society

on the

ninetieth anniversary of its founding

. . . the *Messiah* — executed in so masterly a manner by persons whose hearts as well as their voices and instruments were tuned to the Redeemer's praise, accompanied with the grateful emotions of an audience duly affected with a sense of their obligations to his love — might afford one of the highest and noblest gratifications of which we are capable in the present life.

JOHN NEWTON (1786)

Contents

Illustrations   x

Preface   xi

Three Histories:
"God moves in a mysterious way"

1. Oratorio before Handel   3

   Oratorio in Italy, the Land of Its Birth   3

   Oratorio in Handel's Native Germany   9

   Oratorio in England before Handel   11

2. Handel   12

   Handel before Oratorio in England   12

   Handel and the Origin of Oratorio in England   28

3. *Messiah*   37

   Messiah *during Handel's Lifetime*   37

   Messiah *after Handel's Death*   51

Purpose:
"I wish to make them better"

4. To Teach and Delight   65

5. *Messiah* versus Deism   72

Commentary:
"Great is the mystery of Godliness"

6. Before We Begin   81

    Some General Musical Considerations   81

    Mottoes   84

7. Part the First: The Coming of the Messiah   87

    Scene 1   89

    Scene 2   92

    Scene 3, section 1   97

    Scene 3, section 2   98

    Scene 4   100

    Scene 5   104

8. Part the Second: Lamb of God, King of Kings   108

    Scene 1, prologue   110

    Scene 1, section 1   111

    Scene 1, section 2   114

    Scene 2   118

    Scene 3   121

    Scene 4   123

    Scene 5   124

    Scene 6   127

    Scene 7   129

    Scene 8   134

9. Part the Third: Resurrection of the Dead,
   Worship of the Lamb   140

    Scene 1   141

    Scene 2   144

    Scene 3   145

    Scene 4   147

Contents

Glossary   153

Notes   157

A List of Works Cited   165

Credits   169

Index   170

Illustrations

A Musician (Possibly G. F. Handel), portrait by the English School   1

St. Philip Neri, portrait by Guido Remi   5

Johann Mattheson, mezzotint by J. J. Haid after Wahll   13

Faustina Bordoni, portrait by Rosalba Carriera   23

A Scene from *The Beggar's Opera,* painting by William Hogarth   25

Farinelli, Cuzzoni, and Senesino in *Flavio,* etching by the English School   31

Charles Jennens, portrait by Mason Chamberlain   41

The Foundling Hospital Chapel, lithograph by M. & N. Hanhart
from G. R. Sarjent   47

Monument above Handel's Grave, sculpture by Louis François Roubiliac   52

Messiah Performance at Westminster Abbey   55

The Calvin College Augmented Chorus, 1933   58

The Calvin College Oratorio Society, 2006   61

George Frideric Handel, portrait by Balthasar Denner   63

The Crown and Anchor Tavern, London, drawing by J. Findlay   66

George Frederick Handel, portrait by Thomas Hudson   79

A Page from Handel's Autograph Score of the "Amen" Chorus   151

Preface

Every year, Handel's *Messiah* receives an untold number of performances around the world, often before very large audiences. In my part of the world, the Midwestern United States, they usually take place during Advent; for many, hearing or performing *Messiah* is almost a yearly ritual. And where people cannot attend a live performance, or when they prefer to take their music in the comfort of their own living room, then radio, television, and recordings expand the number of *Messiah* listeners by who knows how many. I recently checked www.archivmusik.com and found eighty-nine recordings of *Messiah* or excerpts from it. Even the number of people who perform *Messiah* is staggering. Rehearsed performances often have choirs whose singers number in the hundreds. Many thousands more, forgoing the rigors of rehearsal, perform *Messiah* at popular sing-alongs. The *Messiah* phenomenon has no parallel in music history. No work of music has survived, let alone thrived, on so many performances, good, bad, and indifferent, by and for so many people, year after year, for such a long time.

Many have tried to explain the phenomenon. Some attempts have been quite imaginative and interesting even as they severely test one's credulity. I heard one explanation claim that the annual trek to hear *Messiah* is a kind of Protestant fertility rite (never mind that for many of us it happens in December!). Most explanations, however, end up saying little more than that Handel, a very good composer, had in Charles Jennens's compilation of Scripture texts an exceptionally fine libretto that inspired him to a peak performance. But that will hardly do to explain the phenomenon that is Handel's *Messiah*. Composers at least as good as Handel who have been as much inspired by great texts have written works that have not received a fraction of the veneration that has been bestowed on *Messiah.*

I am sure that the explanation is to be sought in a complex web of musical, textual, social, religious, and psychological factors that will never be completely unraveled. I am certainly not going to try to unravel it here. My goal is more modest. I simply wish to supply some information, explanation, and interpretation that might enhance appreciation of *Messiah,*

Given the phenomenal popularity of *Messiah,* it might seem that this oratorio, of all pieces of music, is least in need of enhanced appreciation. But I have in mind something different than what is usually meant by appreciation. As Wilson Follett points out, appreciation is used primarily as "a loose synonym of *like, enjoy, approve, take pleasure in.*"[1] So, for example, courses in music appreciation are expected to teach students to "like" or "enjoy" music or, at least, certain kinds of music not customarily associated with students' tastes. Follett is no doubt right in saying that "It is too late now to try to hold *appreciate* to its primary and legitimate meaning: *measure the worth of, put a correct valuation on.*" But that is the meaning I have in mind. It seems to me that *Messiah* is due for some appreciation in the "primary and legitimate" sense of the word; it has had its share of being merely liked. In saying that, I don't mean to suggest that its popularity is undeserved. I certainly don't want to debunk the work or diminish anyone's enjoyment of it by putting a "correct valuation" on it. On the contrary, I am convinced that *Messiah* will be "liked" and "enjoyed" all the more if a "correct valuation" is put on it. Of course, I can say that only because I am convinced of its great worth and the belief that others can more fully recognize its worth through a fuller understanding of the work.

The three sections of this book aim to increase understanding from three different perspectives. The first section traces three histories — the history of oratorio up to *Messiah;* the history of Handel up to *Messiah;* and the history of *Messiah's* inception and reception. Although I think these histories can contribute something toward a greater understanding of the work, I tell them primarily because they reveal a series and confluence of remarkable and unlikely events that led to the making of *Messiah* and from there to the phenomenon that it has become. The story begins with a devotional movement in sixteenth-century Catholic Italy and leads to *Messiah,* an oratorio written by Handel, an eighteenth-century German Lutheran composer who would have preferred to continue writing Italian operas in Protestant England, a country that had no oratorio tradition until he reluctantly "invented" it. The rest, as they say, is history. That oratorio became the phenomenon with which we are all familiar; it has inspired and nourished faith in Jesus of Nazareth, the Messiah, in thousands upon thousands of listeners in the ensuing centuries. As the poet William Cowper wrote, "God moves in a mysterious way, his wonders to perform."

The second section deals with the purposes Charles Jennens had for compiling the libretto of *Messiah* and Handel had for setting it to music. At the beginning of *A Preface to Paradise Lost* C. S. Lewis wrote:

> The first qualification for judging any piece of workmanship from a corkscrew to a cathedral is to know *what* it is — what it was intended to do and how it is meant to be used. After that has been discovered the temperance reformer may decide that the corkscrew was made for a bad purpose, and the communist may think the same about the cathedral. But such questions come later. The first thing is to understand the object before you: as long as you think the corkscrew was meant for opening tins or the cathedral for entertaining tourists you can say nothing to the purpose about them. The first thing the reader needs to know about *Paradise Lost* is what Milton meant it to be.[2]

Messiah has been, and still is, misunderstood in two ways, which can be seen most clearly with reference to a statement the Handel scholar Jens Peter Larsen made about oratorio: "Oratorio acknowledges two masters, the church and the theater."[3] Those who view *Messiah* as sacrosanct are bothered by the suggestion that it pays allegiance to the theater — in other words that it is, and was meant to be, entertainment. On the other hand are those who don't want their entertainment spoiled by the suggestion that it was intended to teach (or worse, preach) something, especially if that something comes from the church.

To get at what *Messiah* was meant to be, the second section first deals with a long-standing theory of art that was still strong in the eighteenth century, but which has since fallen on hard times. It then proceeds from the broad aesthetic background to the more specific purpose Jennens and Handel had in mind for *Messiah.*

The third section turns directly to Jennens's text and Handel's music. It provides commentary on the theological message of the words and the way Handel's music conveys and interprets that message. Jennens provided a wordbook (libretto) for the first London performance in 1743. In it he subdivided its three Parts ("Acts") into scenes, much like the structure of an opera. My commentary follows that structure, but in two cases I have subdivided scenes into smaller sections where I think both text and music warrant it. When quoting Bible texts not in *Messiah,* I have used the King James Version in order to maintain stylistic compatibility with *Messiah* texts. In my description of the music I have avoided technical terminology as much as possible. When I first use a term that is not likely to be widely understood, I give a brief explanation. A glossary also provides definitions of those terms. Reading the commentary is probably best done scene by scene, accompanied by listening either before or after or — best of all — both before and after reading.

I thank my parents, Raymond and Jessie Stapert, for introducing me to *Messiah* through recordings. I thank Seymour Swets and Harold Geerdes, conductors of the Calvin Oratorio Society under whom I had the opportunity to perform *Messiah* as a student, and I thank the conductors who succeeded them — Howard Slenk, Pearl Shangkuan, and Joel Navarro — who have continued the tradition and provided me with yearly opportunities to hear *Messiah.* Ruth Van Baak Griffioen and Michael Marissen did me great service by reading an entire draft of this book. I thank them both for making the book better.

Finally, though this hardly completes the list of those to whom I am indebted, I thank Jon Pott, Linda Bieze, and Klaas Wolterstorff of Eerdmans — Jon for valuable suggestions and encouragement during the book's conceptual stage, Linda for the final editorial work and picture research, and Klaas for the book's graphic design.

Three Histories

"God moves in a mysterious way"

A Musician (possibly G. F. Handel). Oil on canvas, English School (18th century), Fitzwilliam Museum, University of Cambridge, U.K.

Chapter 1

Oratorio before Handel

Oratorio in Italy, the Land of Its Birth

A "polite assembly" crowded into Dublin's music hall in Fishamble Street on 10 April 1742 for a public rehearsal of an upcoming concert. Those attending the rehearsal had tickets for the formal concert scheduled for two days later, but their tickets entitled them to attend the rehearsal also. The concert was postponed one day to 13 April because certain "persons of distinction" so desired. Despite the postponement and the fact that many had already heard the rehearsal, an estimated seven hundred people shoehorned themselves into the six hundred-seat music hall. (Obviously, the ladies and gentlemen heeded the request of the advertisements to come without skirt hoops and swords.) Thus began the remarkable history of one of the most well-received works in the annals of music. But no less remarkable than the initial reception of the work advertised as "Mr. Handel's new Grand Oratorio, call'd the MESSIAH" is the unlikely series of events that led to its composition.

Oratorio is a difficult genre to define. Handel scholar Winton Dean said, "It is almost impossible to define it without excluding famous works that go or have gone in the catalogue of oratorios."[1] But all oratorios have one element in common. Like operas, they are dramatic stories entirely set to music for vocal soloists, chorus, and instruments. But unlike operas, they do not usually include acting, costumes, and stage props. Also unlike opera, oratorios usually tell sacred stories drawn from the Old Testament or lives of early Christian saints.

Both opera and oratorio originated and developed in Italy during the late Renaissance and early Baroque periods in music history (roughly the late sixteenth and early seventeenth centuries), a time of increasing interest in setting dramatic texts to music. That interest gave rise to the "invention" of opera at the turn of the seventeenth century, and oratorio, opera's sacred counterpart, followed in its wake. The same musical styles and techniques that early seventeenth-century opera composers developed for telling the stories of heroes of ancient mythology and history became used in oratorio to tell the stories of early Christian saints and biblical characters, especially heroic figures from the Old Testament and the Apocrypha, such as Samson, Deborah, Susanna, and Judas Maccabeus.

The earliest such works came to be called oratorios because they were performed in oratories, or prayer halls, that developed out of a devotional movement led by St. Philip Neri (1515-1595) during the Catholic Counter Reformation. The meetings he instigated in the 1550s were at first small and informal. A few men met to pray, to discuss spiritual matters, and, since Neri considered singing an important spiritual exercise, to sing. These meetings soon became popular. Increasing attendance necessitated larger meeting places — oratories that could hold a few hundred people. The meetings developed into devotional and instructional services for the laity that included sermons preached in the vernacular.

Music continued to be an important part of the proceedings. Much of it came from the repertory of *laude,* simple religious songs in the vernacular whose origins go back to the penitential fervor that swept Italy in the last half of the thirteenth century, prompted to a large extent by the activity of St. Francis of Assisi and his followers. Much of the *lauda* repertory was suitable for congregational singing, but professional musicians performed the more sophisticated polyphonic *laude* as well as motets and madrigals with sacred subjects *(madrigale spirituali),* especially for the more elaborate services that took place in oratories on special occasions after Vespers *(oratorio vespertino).* Some motets and spiritual madrigals, and even some of the newer *laude,* had dramatic texts. But however dramatic the texts might have been, the music sung in the oratories would not have led to oratorio had it not been for the concurrent development of opera in the secular realm.

St. Philip Neri, leader of the sixteenth-century devotional movement out of which oratorio developed. Portrait by Guido Remi (1575-1642), S. Maria in Vallicella (Chiesa Nuova), Rome, Italy.

Composers in Florence, Italy, at the end of the sixteenth century made opera and oratorio possible when they developed a new style of solo singing called *stile rappresentativo* ("representative style"). It consisted of a solo voice accompanied by basso continuo — that is, a bass instrument (such as cello or bassoon) and a keyboard or plucked stringed instrument (such as harpsichord, organ, or lute) to fill out the harmonies between the bass instrument and the solo voice. Solo singing with basso continuo accompaniment could cross a wide continuum of styles ranging from speech-like declamation to melodious, often florid, lyricism. The declamatory end of the continuum was essential for opera. It "represented" human speech and made it possible to sing dramatic dialogue. (The declamatory style soon became called "recitative," that is, a "reciting" style. The name has stuck.)

The earliest opera we know of is *Dafne*, composed by Jacopo Peri (1561-1633) and first performed in Florence in 1598. Most of the music is lost, however. Soon after *Dafne*, Peri composed *Eurydice*, the first extant opera. It was first performed in 1600, again in Florence. Sixteen hundred was also the year of the first performance of another large-scale, fully sung musical drama — *Rappresentatione di Anima, et di Corpo (The Representation of the Soul and the Body)*. Since staging suggestions were included in the preface (though it's not clear to what extent the performance was staged), *Rappresentatione* has often been referred to as a sacred opera, but its moralizing subject and its performance with interspersed short sermons in the oratory of Neri's Chiesa Nuova in Rome put it more in line with oratorio. However, it had no immediate successors and remained one of a kind. Nevertheless, it marked an important step in the linking of sacred, or quasi-sacred, subject matter with dramatic music.

More direct forerunners of oratorios are certain sacred works by other composers working in Rome in the early seventeenth century who composed collections of music explicitly intended for use in oratories. Giovanni Francesco Anerio composed a collection dedicated to the memory of Neri, who, as the dedication states, used the sweetness of music to attract people to the devotional services in oratories. Most of the texts in these collections are dramatic. More important, several of them are dramatic dialogues whose musical settings are nearly as extensive and dramatically conceived as the works the next generation would call oratorios.

As the devotional services in oratories became more popular, the music became more elaborate. Stories from the Old Testament and saints' lives became the favored subject matter. In 1639 a French traveler to Rome described a musical performance he heard in the oratory of the Arciconfraternita del Crocifisso in the Church of San Marcello.

> On two sides of the church there were two other little galleries, in which were placed some of the most excellent instrumentalists. The voices would begin with a psalm in the form of a motet, and then all the instruments would play a very good symphony. The voices would sing a story from the Old Testament, a form of a spiritual play, for example that of Susanna, of Judith and Holofernes, or of David and Goliath. Each singer represented one person of the story and expressed perfectly the force of the words.[2]

The Frenchman's description of the singing of "a story from the Old Testament" in the "form of a spiritual play" suggests that what he heard was an early oratorio.

Perhaps the best of the early Italian composers of oratorio was Giacomo Carissimi (1605-1674). He worked his entire career in Rome and its environs, most of it as *maestro di cappella* at the Collegio Germanico e Ungarico, a Jesuit seminary. He was responsible for the music at the church of Sant' Apollinare; he was also involved with the music of the oratories, especially the Arciconfraternita del Crocifisso visited by the aforementioned French traveler.

Carissimi's *Jephte* offers a typical, and especially fine, example of the early Italian oratorio. Its libretto is an expanded paraphrase of the story from Judges 11:28-38 in which Jephthah vows to offer as a burnt offering to the Lord whatever comes out from his house to meet him when he returns from war with the Ammonites. After the Lord gives him victory, the first to come out to meet him is his daughter, dancing with tambourines.

The story is told by a narrator, "historicus," whose words are sung by various soloists, ensembles, and chorus. The words of Jephthah and his daughter are sung by tenor and soprano soloists respectively. The accompaniment requires only basso continuo, but using other instruments to double the voices in the choruses was probably customary.

In addition to telling the story quite directly from the book of Judges, the librettist composed additional poetry to flesh it out: a battle song sung first by a bass soloist (a warrior) and then by the chorus (the army); a victory song sung first by Jephthah's daughter, then by two sopranos (her companions), and finally by the choir (the people of Israel); Jephthah's daughter's lament in the mountains, with additional voices providing effectively haunting echoes; and the lament of the "daughters of Israel" who "went year by year to lament the daughter of Jephthah the Gileadite four days in the year." The bare story provided Carissimi with a highly dramatic situation and some emotionally charged dialogue between Jephthah and his daughter. The librettist's additions gave Carissimi opportunities to write some of the stock types of music that would be expected in an opera — in this case battle music, a celebratory victory song, and laments. Carissimi "painted" all the dramatic moments in broad, sure musical strokes, but the final choral lament is the gem of the piece, worthy to be placed alongside Henry Purcell's great lament for Dido at the end of his opera *Dido and Aeneas*.

By the end of Carissimi's life, oratorio was a flourishing genre that had spread from Rome to other Italian cities and was being performed not only in oratories but in such venues as educational institutions and private palaces. Among the many composers who contributed to the genre were Bernardo Pasquini, Alessandro Stradella, and Alessandro Scarlatti, hardly household names today, but worthy composers nonetheless. Oratorio also spread to Catholic centers beyond Italy like Dresden and Vienna. It was still being cultivated in the late eighteenth century by, among others, Antonio Salieri, whose undeserved present-day notoriety and reputation for mediocrity are due to the film version of Peter Shafer's play *Amadeus*.

Handel encountered Italian oratorios when he was a young composer working in Italy. He contributed two works to the repertory, *Il trionfo del Tempo e del Disinganno (The Triumph of Time and Truth)* and *La Resurrezione (The Resurrection)*.

Oratorio in Handel's Native Germany

In Handel's homeland during the seventeenth century, musical settings of Bible stories, like the Italian oratorios, used the new musical styles and techniques the Italians had developed in opera. But textually and functionally, the German works of the seventeenth century that we usually refer to as oratorios remained outside the Italian orbit. They belong to a genre more properly called *historia*, which has its roots in the ancient Roman Catholic liturgical practice of chanting the Gospel accounts of the Passion story during Holy Week. Lutheran *historiae*, with their roots firmly embedded in that pre-Reformation liturgical practice, retained the exact words from the Bible and a close connection to the liturgy. Unlike the Italian oratorios with their newly written re-telling of heroic stories from the Old Testament, *historia* texts told the stories of Christ's birth, passion, resurrection, or ascension directly from Luther's translation of the New Testament. Liturgically they functioned as Scripture readings. Heinrich Schütz (1585-1672) was the first great Lutheran composer to contribute to the *historia* tradition. His settings of the Christmas, Passion, and Resurrection stories are unsurpassed examples of early Lutheran *historiae*. Handel's contemporary, J. S. Bach (1685-1750) was the last great Lutheran composer to cultivate *historiae*, but by his time the generic name had changed to oratorio (except for the Passions), and chorale texts and newly composed devotional poetry were added to the prose accounts from the Bible. Nevertheless, with their specific liturgical function and their retention of narrative directly from the Gospel accounts, Bach's Passions and Christmas Oratorio are best understood as *historiae*.

We do not know what Handel knew of the German *historiae*, though it seems likely that he would have heard some of them in his youth since he was born and raised a Lutheran. But he never was an employee of a Lutheran church, so he had no occasion to write such works, and they seem to have had little influence on his own oratorio composition. He was, however, acquainted with a new type of German oratorio that began in the early eighteenth century, a type that owed much to Italian influence. According to historian of oratorio Howard Smither, during the first decade of the eighteenth century the term *oratorio,* or *Oratorium,* began to be used in print in Protestant Germany to refer to German works. In 1704 the poet Christian Friedrich Hunold . . . used the term on the title page of the printed libretto of his Passion oratorio, which was set to music by Reinhard Keiser, *Der blutige und sterbende Jesus, wie selbiger in einem Oratorio musikalisch geset . . .* ("The Bloody and Dying Jesus, As the Same [Is] Set Musically in an Oratorio . . ."). Two years later, when Hunold published his oratorio text in a collection of his poems, he made clear the Italian influence by describing the work as being "in verses throughout, and without the Evangelist [an essential ingredient in *historiae*], just like the Italian so-called *Oratorien.*"[3]

Handel was twenty years old and living in Hamburg when Keiser's *Der blutige und sterbende Jesus* was first performed.

These eighteenth-century German oratorios paraphrased the literal biblical account of the story and surrounded it with poetry of highly emotional character. They were performed as concert, not liturgical, music although records indicate performances in churches as well as in secular venues. Even though they were quite popular from the beginning, they drew criticism wherever they were performed. When Keiser's *Der blutige und sterbende Jesus* was performed in a church it was faulted for substituting poetic paraphrase for the literal biblical text and for being too theatrical. Other oratorios provoked similar complaints. Concerning one of them the Hamburg senate said that it was a work "so constituted, that it has flowed much more from the spirit of opera than from God's Word, for the Holy Spirit does not know such a method, and we find it nowhere in the revealed divine words that one should treat the sacred story in such a theatrical manner."[4]

But these same oratorios were not above criticism when performed in secular venues either. Keiser's *Der blutige und sterbende Jesus,* when mounted on a stage in a poorhouse, disturbed some of the citizens of Hamburg because a devotional work was performed in secular surroundings and admission was charged.

Since a *St. John Passion* that was once attributed to Handel is spurious, Handel's lone contribution to German oratorio is a setting of the

Passion by the poet Barthold Heinrich Brockes. Its text, which proved to be very popular with composers, abounds in "extravagant images used for their sensational, shocking effect."[5] We know of settings by Telemann, Matheson, Keiser, and Fasch. We know nothing about the circumstances that brought about Handel's setting. He composed it in England, perhaps as early as 1716, but the earliest performance for which we have documentation took place in the refectory of the Hamburg Cathedral during Lent in 1719. Handel's setting of Brockes's text has received mixed reviews. But whatever the overall quality of this youthful work, it contains some wonderful music. Winton Dean's assessment is typical: "Handel's most substantial setting of his native language, though inventive and mature in style, is not an artistic success. . . . The dramatic episodes, especially the Gethsemane scene, are splendidly realized, but the numerous commentary arias lack conviction."[6]

Oratorio in England before Handel

In England, the country where Handel spent most of his creative life, native opera had little chance to take root due to Puritan opposition during a critical time in opera's development elsewhere. Since oratorio generally flourished where opera did, it is not surprising that oratorio did not exist in England before Handel. The only sacred dramatic music was the dialogue, an outgrowth of the verse anthem. It originated in the early seventeenth century, at the same time as similar works in Italy, with pieces like *King Solomon and the Two Harlots* and *The Dialogue of Job, God, Satan, Job's Wife, and the Messengers,* both by John Hilton (d. 1608). But the genre never flourished. Henry Purcell (1659-1695), England's greatest composer in the generation immediately preceding Handel, wrote only one sacred dialogue, *In Guilty Night,* based on the story of King Saul and the Witch of Endor. So there was no oratorio tradition in England before Handel arrived — or for several years thereafter. English oratorio would be his "invention."

Chapter 2

Handel

Handel before Oratorio in England

George Frideric Handel (1685-1759), born into a Lutheran family in Halle, Germany, received his early musical training from Friedrich Wilhelm Zachau, organist and composer at the Liebfrauenkirche in that city. In 1702, in accordance with his parents' wishes, he enrolled at the University of Halle to study law. But by 1703 he was in Hamburg, playing in the opera orchestra, first as violinist, then as harpsichordist. The Hamburg Opera was under the direction of Reinhard Keiser, Germany's leading opera composer at the time.

In August 1703 Handel traveled with his friend and fellow musician Johann Mattheson to Lübeck to investigate the prospect of an opening for the prestigious position of organist at the Marienkirche. That position was then held by the most famous organist of the day, the aging Dieterich Buxtehude. Both Handel and Mattheson (like J. S. Bach two years later) lost interest in the position when they learned that the new organist was expected to marry Buxtehude's daughter, who was no longer in the bloom of youth and apparently not very attractive. Had Handel taken that position, his career would have been set on a very different course from the one it actually took. But it seems unlikely that his interest was very strong, even apart from the marriage requirement. Probably his interest in opera had brought him to Hamburg in the first place. Even if it hadn't, his career turned decidedly in the direction of opera during his time there. While living there he composed his first two operas, *Almira* and *Nero,* both performed early in 1705.

Johann Mattheson, Handel's friend and fellow musician. Mezzotint by J. J. Haid after Wahll (1741), Gerald Coke Collection, The Foundling Museum, London, England.

According to John Mainwaring (1724-1807), Handel's first biographer, in Hamburg Handel became acquainted with "the Prince of Tuscany, brother to John Gaston de Medicis, Grand Duke."

The Prince was a great lover of the art for which his country is so renowned. Handel's proficiency in it, not only procured him access to his Highness, but occasioned a sort of intimacy betwixt them: they frequently discoursed on the state of Music in general, and on the merits of Composers, Singers, and Performers in particular. The Prince would often lament that Handel was not acquainted with those of Italy; shewed him a large collection of Italian Music; and was very desirous he should return with him to Florence.[1]

Handel, however, seems to have played hard to get, showing in the process some youthful and nationalistic arrogance. He "plainly confessed that he could see nothing in the Music which answered the high character his Highness had given it." Even though the prince "assured him that there was no country in which a young proficient could spend his time to so much advantage . . . Handel replied, that if this were so, he was much at a loss to conceive how such great culture should be followed by so little fruit." The Prince merely "smiled" and said "that there needed nothing but a journey to reconcile him to the style and taste which prevailed there." Handel's interest was obviously aroused, but given his "noble spirit of independency" (read "Saxon stubbornness"?), he turned down the invitation to go to Italy with the Prince despite being promised that "no conveniences should be wanting." Instead "he resolved to go to Italy on his own bottom, as soon as he could make a purse for that occasion."[2]

Handel's itinerary in Italy (1706-1710) is not clear, but we know he found support from patrons in Rome — Cardinals Pamphili and Ottoboni, and Marquis Ruspoli. Naturally enough he wrote some Catholic church music — *Dixit Dominus, Laudate pueri,* and *Nisi Dominus* — and, as already noted, two oratorios — *Il trionfo del Tempo e del Disinganno (The Triumph of Time and Truth)* and *La Resurrezione (The Resurrection). Il Trionfo,* an allegorical morality play, was first performed in 1707. *La Resurrezione* followed a year later. It was written for Marquis Ruspoli and performed in his palace on Easter Sunday following a performance the previous Wednesday of a Passion oratorio by Alessandro Scarlatti. Although not acted, Handel's oratorio was performed against a large painted background depicting, in the words of its painter, Angelo Cerruti, "the resurrection of our Lord with a gloria of *putti* [cherubs] and cherubim, and the angel sitting on the tomb announcing the resurrection to Mary Magdalene and Mary Cleopha, with John the Evangelist in the vicinity of a mountain, and demons pounging into the abyss."[3] For the performance Handel had an impressive orchestra to work with — twenty violins, four violas, six cellos, five string basses, one bass viol, four oboes, two trumpets, and a trombone. The conductor was none other than the great violinist-composer Archangelo Corelli!

Most of his time in Italy was devoted to composing secular Italian cantatas. Since these cantatas were similar to operatic scenes in both textual content and musical style, they provided good stepping-stones to his composition of full-fledged operas. The cantatas also served as convenient sources of musical plunder for his operas. Although he wrote only two operas while in Italy, *Roderigo* and *Agrippina,* they — especially *Agrippina* — already show that Handel possessed an exceptional talent with a flare for the stage.

Handel's reputation as a harpsichordist and organist must have preceded him to Italy. In Venice, Mainwaring tells us, "He was first discovered . . . at a Masquerade, while he was playing on a harpsichord in his visor. [Domenico] Scarlatti happened to be there, and affirmed that it could be no one but the famous Saxon, or the devil."[4] At another time a keyboard contest was arranged between Handel and Scarlatti.

The issue of the trial on the harpsichord hath been differently reported. It has been said that some gave the preference to Scarlatti. However, when they came to the Organ there was not the least pretence for doubting to which of them it belonged. Scarlatti himself declared the superiority of his antagonist, and owned ingenuously, that till he had heard him upon this instrument, he had no conception of its powers.[5]

On 26 December 1709, Handel's second Italian opera, *Agrippina,* a satirical comedy, opened the carnival season in Venice. It was a great success. Because the carnival audience was international, the success of the opera did much to spread Handel's growing reputation. During this time he probably met Prince Ernst Georg and was invited to come to Hanover. Ernst Georg was the brother of Elector George Ludwig of Hanover, the future King George I of England. Handel went to Hanover in 1710, and already by 16 June he had been offered a position as *Kapellmeister* to the court of Elector George Ludwig. However, he had two previous commitments to fulfill. According to Mainwaring, Handel "expressed his apprehensions that the favour intended him would hardly be consistent either with the promise he had actually made to visit the courts of the Elector Palatine, or with the resolution he had long taken to pass over into England, for the sake of seeing London." But George Ludwig gave him "leave to be absent for a twelvemonth or more if he chose it; and to go whithersoever he pleased. On these easy conditions he thankfully accepted [the appointment]."[6] Given the Elector's generous provision for being away, Handel first went to Düsseldorf and then, in the autumn of 1710, to London.

Opera in England at that time was in a confused state. The masque had been an important musical-dramatic art form in England during the early seventeenth century, and it seems likely that English opera would have developed out of the masque during that century, much as French opera had developed out of ballet. But in 1642, under the increasing influence of the Puritans, theaters in London were closed, and they remained closed until the Commonwealth ended in 1660. Obviously, the closure of the theaters at that crucial time hindered the development of English opera. But it didn't entirely close the door. Masques continued to be performed in private, and some proto-operas apparently were performed publicly. As historian of opera Donald Grout explains, "The Puritans had not aimed to suppress secular music, but they did oppose the theatre, and this resulted in an attempt to evade their prohibition by disguising a theatrical spectacle as a musical concert."[7] One such work, perhaps the first English opera, was *The Siege of Rhodes,* performed in 1656. Its music, now lost, was written by several composers, and it was disguised by being publicized as "A Representation by the art of Prospective Scenes and the Story sung in Recitative Musick." So English opera might have continued to develop in spite of the ban on theatrical productions.

But a curious thing happened as a result of the Restoration: the removal of the prohibition against stage plays actually put a stop to opera. Again Grout explains:

> English audiences preferred spoken drama, and once this was permitted they no longer had any interest in maintaining a form which to them represented only a makeshift, called forth by special circumstances. Theatre music, to be sure, was composed after the Restoration, but not in the form of opera; it was confined for the most part to masques and incidental music for plays. . . .[8]

Only two English works of the late seventeenth century can be truly classified as operas, John Blow's *Venus and Adonis* and Henry Purcell's *Dido and Aeneas.* Had Purcell lived to write more operas, they might have become the foundation on which English opera could build. But Purcell died at the youthful age of thirty-six. English opera had to wait until the twentieth century for a comparable talent.

So except for the handful of seventeenth-century examples, opera in England was barely five years old when Handel arrived in London. Two rival theaters figured principally in the introduction of opera. One was the Theatre Royal in Drury Lane, one of the original patent theaters licensed to stage dramas after the Restoration under Charles II in 1660. The other was the newly constructed Queen's (later King's) Theatre in the Haymarket, which opened on 9 April 1705 with an opera by Jacob Greber that was sung partly in English, partly in Italian. But Drury Lane had already beaten the Queen's Theatre to the punch three months earlier with an all-English opera by Thomas Clayton on 16 January. Neither was very successful. A contemporary account of the Haymarket opening of Greber's opera reads:

> And upon the *9th,* of *April,* 1705. Captain *Vanbrugg* open'd his new Theatre in the *Hay-Market,* with a Foreign Opera, Perform'd by a new set of Singers, Arriv'd from *Italy;* (the worst that e'er came

from thence) for it lasted but 5 Days, and they being lik'd but indifferently by the Gentry; they in a little time marcht back to their own Country.[9]

However, an English version of *Camilla* by the Italian composer Giovanni Bononcini was very successful when performed at Drury Lane.

> . . . the Theatre in *Drury-Lane* Presented the Opera of *Camilla*, Compos'd by *Gio. Buononcini*, and prepared for the *English* Stage, by *Ni[col]o Ha[y]m*; this being a Royal Opera, the Musick admirable, and Perform'd in a more regular Method than any of the former (tho' much of its Beauty was lost in the *English* Language) it receiv'd so Universal an Applause, that I don't think it ever met with so good a Reception in any of its first Representations Abroad.[10]

In 1706 the managers of the Drury Lane and Haymarket theaters reached an agreement: opera would be performed at Drury Lane and spoken drama at the Haymarket. But in 1708 the Lord Chamberlain reversed that arrangement. So when Handel arrived in London for the first time in 1710, the Queen's Theatre in the Haymarket was the place for opera, and by that time the fashion had turned entirely in favor of Italian opera.

Handel wasted no time getting involved in London's fledgling operatic scene with the composition of *Rinaldo*. It opened on 24 February 1711 (the day after his twenty-sixth birthday), the first Italian opera by any composer written specifically for production in England. Its libretto is based on episodes from one of the great epic poems of the Renaissance, Tasso's *Gerusalemme liberate (Jerusalem Liberated)*, and its staging was especially spectacular, though lampooned by Joseph Addison. In an essay in *The Spectator* he tells of an encounter with "an ordinary fellow carrying a cage full of sparrows upon his shoulders." This fellow told a friend that he was collecting them for the opera.

> Sparrows for the opera! Says his friend, licking his lips; what, are they to be roasted? No, no, says the other; they are to enter towards the end of the first act, and to fly about the stage.

This strange dialogue awakened my curiosity so far, that I immediately bought [the libretto of] the opera, by means of which I ascertained the sparrows were to act the part of singing birds in a delightful grove. . . . At the same time I made this discovery, I found . . . it had been proposed to break down a part of the wall, and to surprise the audience with a party of an hundred horse; and that there was actually a project of bringing the New River into the house, to be employed in jetteaus and water-works. This project, as I have since heard, is postponed till the summer season; when it is thought the coolness that proceeds from fountains and cascades will be more acceptable and refreshing to people of quality. In the meantime, to find out a more agreeable entertainment for the winter season, the opera of *Rinaldo* is filled with thunder and lightning, illuminations and fireworks; which the audience may look upon without catching cold, and indeed without much danger of being burnt; for there are several engines filled with water, and ready to play at a minute's warning, in case any such accident should happen. However, as I have a very great friendship for the owner of the theatre, I hope that he has been wise enough to insure his house before he would let this opera be acted in it. . . .

But to return to the sparrows; there have been so many flights of them let loose in this opera, that it is feared the house will never get rid of them; and that in other plays they make their entrance in very wrong and improper scenes so as to be seen flying in a lady's bed-chamber, or perching upon a king's throne; besides the inconveniences which the heads of the audience may sometimes suffer from them.[11]

Addison's satire notwithstanding, a total of fifteen performances indicates that *Rinaldo* was an exceptionally popular success.

After a brief visit to Germany, Handel returned to London in the fall of 1712 and would make it his home for the rest of his life. Queen Anne gave him a pension even though he was still in the employ of the Elector of Hanover and was not an English citizen. It was not until 1727 that he became a naturalized citizen of England by one of the final official acts of King George I. When he was the Elector of Hanover,

George I had been Handel's employer. He succeeded Queen Anne as English sovereign after she died because he was her closest living Protestant relative. Even though she had many closer English relatives, they could not succeed her because the 1701 Act of Settlement prohibited Catholics from inheriting the throne of England.

During the next few seasons at the King's Theatre in the Haymarket, Handel mounted repeat performances of *Rinaldo* and composed *Il pastor fido (The Faithful Shepherd), Teseo, Silla,* and *Amadigi.* Only *Teseo* (with thirteen performances) came close to the popularity of *Rinaldo.* During those years, financial and managerial problems threatened the future of opera at the King's Theatre, but perhaps the chief factor that led to its termination in 1717 was "a political and social division among its patrons."

> [A] family row . . . broke out between the king and the Prince of Wales at the christening of Prince George William in November 1717, which resulted in the banishment of the Prince and Princess of Wales from St. James's Palace and their separation from their children, who were retained by the king. This crisis was . . . the culmination of a political process involving the growth of an opposition party that had been gathering around the Prince of Wales in the preceding months. The success of the opera company relied on a patronage base which, if not actually politically united, could at least sink its social divisions temporarily: this was not possible when attendance at the courts of the king and the Prince of Wales became mutually exclusive.[12]

Opera in the King's Theatre would return in a couple of years, but in the meantime Handel found a patron, James Brydges, Earl of Carnarvon, soon to be Duke of Chandos. His principal compositions during this time were the eleven so-called Chandos Anthems and two masques, *Acis and Galatea* and one on a sacred subject, *Haman and Mordecai* (which, renamed *Esther,* would later become his first English oratorio). During this hiatus from opera, writing these compositions gave him experience in areas that would be important when he eventually turned to oratorio — setting English texts to music and writing for choir. Until now he had very little experience in setting English texts, and choral music was negligible to non-existent in Italian opera.

In 1719 a group of aristocrats, including the Duke of Chandos, desiring to bring Italian opera back to the King's Theatre in the Haymarket, formed the Royal Academy of Music. This was a joint stock company, but its financial support also included one thousand pounds a year promised by King George I. With the king's patronage plus an initial list of about sixty subscribers, the new company had a reasonably firm financial foundation, though of course it would still need box-office success to survive. Handel was appointed "Master of the Orchestra" and would be the principal composer. He traveled to Italy to engage singers and composed *Radamisto* for the first season. It was first performed on 27 April and received nine further performances before the season closed in June.

The King's Theatre thrived for the next several years, and Handel was very productive. He composed twelve more operas before the end of the 1727-1728 season. Most of them received at least ten performances; two, *Admeto* and *Siroe*, were performed nineteen and eighteen times respectively. Included among these operas are three of his greatest — *Giulio Cesare, Tamerlano,* and *Rodelinda* — written for the 1723-1724 and 1724-1725 seasons, the high point of opera at the King's Theatre.

Handel was highly revered by many (though he had detractors and enemies too), and his operas were generally successful. But the overall success of all the operas (not just Handel's) produced at the King's Theatre by the Royal Academy varied, and since opera is an extravagant art form, and therefore expensive, varying success will not keep it financially afloat. The fees of star Italian singers contributed significantly to the expense of opera. Furthermore, since these stars developed their own followers (often quite rabid), they split audiences into rival factions. Their egos also caused problems, both among themselves and with management. That became an acute problem for the Royal Academy when they added a second female star to their roster in 1726. The celebrated Faustina debuted in Handel's *Alessandro* alongside the equally celebrated Cuzzoni, who had been the *prima donna* in the company since her debut in January 1723. Although Handel carefully balanced their roles, friction developed between the two *prime donne*

— two *prime* being a mathematical impossibility. It escalated during the following year and came to a climax at a performance of an opera by Bononcini on 6 June 1727. On 10 June the *British Journal* reported:

> On Tuesday-night last, a great Disturbance happened at the Opera, occasioned by the Partisans of the Two Celebrated Rival Ladies, Cuzzoni and Faustina. The Contention at first was only carried on by Hissing on one Side, and Clapping on the other; but proceeded at length to Catcalls, and other great Indecencies: And notwithstanding the Princess Caroline was present, no Regards were of Force to restrain the Rudenesses of the Opponents.[13]

The press and pamphleteers had a heyday keeping the incident in the public consciousness and probably spicing it up a bit. A satirical essay, "The Devil to Pay at St. James's" (included in a collection of pieces by Handel's friend Dr. John Arbuthnot, but not written by him), begins:

> Two of a trade seldom or ever agree: This we daily see verified in the many Skirmishes between the Ladies that sell Mackrel near *London-Bridge,* and the Nymphs that vend live Mutton about *Fleet-Street* and *Covent-Garden:* But who would have thought the Infection should reach the *Hay-market,* and inspire Two Singing Ladies to pull each other's Coiffs, to the no small Disquiet of the Directors, who (God help them) have enough to keep Peace and Quietness between them.

The author wrote that he would not "determine who is the Aggressor, but take the surer Side, and wisely pronounce them both in Fault; for it is certainly an apparent Shame that two such well bred ladies should call Bitch and Whore, should scold and fight like any Billingsgates."[14]

Exaggerated in the press or not, the squabble brought an end to the 1726-1727 season. The Royal Academy held on for one more season but folded in 1728. So less than two decades after *Rinaldo* debuted, opera productions by the Royal Academy ceased due to financial woes

Italian mezzo-soprano Faustina Bordoni (1697-1781) made her London debut in Handel's opera *Alessandro* alongside a rival *prima donna*. Portrait by Rosalba Carriera (1675-1757), Museo del Settecento Veniziano, Ca' Rezzonico, Venice, Italy.

and internal personnel problems. Waning audiences no longer provided sufficient revenue to sustain the productions. The attrition was no doubt the result of weariness with listening to two or three hours of music in a foreign language — "nonsense well-tun'd" (in the memorable phrase of Thomas Tickell in his poem "To [Joseph Addison] the Author of Rosamond"). Indeed, we might wonder how opera in a foreign language remained popular as long as it did and even ask why a fashion for Italian opera took hold in England in the first place.

Some of the English questioned it themselves. Addison wondered about it from the outset. Already in 1711 he wrote a characteristically witty essay in *The Spectator* about Italian opera on the English stage. He wrote it because he was sure that "our great Grand-children will be very curious to know the Reason why their Forefathers used to sit together like an Audience of Foreigners in their own Country, and to hear whole Plays acted before them in a Tongue which they did not understand." He called it a "monstrous practice" made fashionable by "the Poetasters and Fiddlers" who "laid down as an established rule. . . . *[that] nothing is capable of being well set to Musick, that is not Nonsense.*"[15]

Undoubtedly, a complex of social factors contributed to establishing the fashion; likewise, a complex of social factors contributed to its waning. In addition to their weariness with, in the words of Samuel Johnson, "exotick and irrational entertainment"[16] many were also growing weary of stories of heroes from the distant past and the high Baroque musical styles to which they were set. So it is no surprise that in 1728 an opera was produced in London that met all three sources of dissatisfaction head on. *The Beggar's Opera*, with a libretto by John Gay (1685-1732) and music arranged by Johann Christoph Pepusch (1667-1752), is in English instead of Italian, it is filled with characters from eighteenth-century London's seamier districts instead of heroes of the distant past, and it alternates between spoken dialogue and catchy, popular tunes instead of recitatives and arias. (*The Three-penny Opera* of Bertolt Brecht and Kurt Weill is based on *The Beggar's Opera*.)

The opera premiered at the Lincoln's Inn Fields, a theater managed by John Rich. It was enormously successful — an "unexampled success" in the words of Samuel Johnson, who quoted the wag who re-

A scene from *The Beggar's Opera*, one of the first English-language operas, by Johann Christoph Pepusch and John Gay. Oil on canvas by William Hogarth, 1731, Tate Gallery, London, England.

marked that it "made Gay *rich* and Rich *gay*."[17] A note in Alexander Pope's *Dunciad* regarding its first performance says, "The piece was received with greater applause than was ever known." The note goes on:

> Besides being acted in London sixty-three days without interruption and renewed next season with equal applause, it spread to all the great towns of England; was played in many places to the thirtieth and fortieth time; at Bath and Bristol, fifty. It made its progress into Wales, Scotland and Ireland, where it was performed twenty-four days successively. The ladies carried about with them the favorite songs of it in fans, and houses were furnished with it in screens. The person who acted Polly, till then obscure, became all at once the favourite of the town; her pictures were engraved and sold in great numbers; her Life written, books of letters and verses

to her published, and pamphlets made even of her sayings and jests. Furthermore, it drove out of England (for the season) the Italian Opera, which had carried all before it for ten years.[18]

A poem in the 13 April 1728 issue of the *Craftsman* exalts Lavinia Fenton (who played Polly) over the star Italian singers in Handel's operas.

> Of all the Belles that tread the Stage,
>   There's none like pretty *Polly*,
> And all the Musick of the Age,
>   Except her Voice, is Folly.

> Compar'd with her, how flat appears
>   *Cuzzoni* or *Faustina?*
> And when she sings, I shut my Ears
>   To warbling *Senesino*.

It ends by accusing "Partizans of *Handel*" of spreading rumors about her.

> Some Prudes indeed, with envious Spight
>   Would blast her Reputation,
> And tell us that to *Ribands* bright
>   She yields, upon Occasion.

> But these are all invented Lies,
>   And vile outlandish Scandal,
> Which from *Italian* Clubs arise,
>   And Partizans of *Handel*.[19]

Although the note in *The Dunciad* claimed that *The Beggar's Opera* "drove out of England (for that season) the Italian Opera, which had carried all before it for ten years," Handel and Italian opera still had supporters. Some of them publicly expressed their dismay over the popularity of *The Beggar's Opera*. Mrs. Pendarves, a friend of Handel, wrote to her sister: "Yesterday I was at the rehearsal of the new opera composed by Handel: I like it extremely, but the taste of the town is so depraved, that nothing will be approved of but the burlesque. The Beggars' Opera entirely triumphs over the Italian one."[20] And the *London Journal* printed a letter saying, "As there is nothing which surprizes all true Lovers of Music more, than the Neglect into which the *Italian* Operas are at present fallen; so I cannot but think it a very extraordinary Instance of the fickle and inconstant Temper of the *English* Nation."[21]

The competition for audience between Italian opera and "ballad opera" (the generic designation for *The Beggar's Opera* and its ilk) was not solely aesthetic — "high brow" versus "low brow" to use later terms. The issue also featured a moral dimension, outlined by Samuel Johnson:

> [Jonathan] Swift commended it [*The Beggar's Opera*] for the excellence of its morality, as a piece that *placed all kinds of vice in the strongest and most odious light;* but others, and among them Dr. Herring, afterwards Archbishop of Canterbury, censured it as giving encouragement, not only to vice, but to crimes, by making a highwayman the hero and dismissing him at last unpunished. It has been even said that after the exhibition of the *Beggar's Opera* the gangs of robbers were evidently multiplied.[22]

Johnson's best known remark on the subject suggests that he was much nearer to Dr. Herring's position than to Swift's: "There is in it [*The Beggar's Opera*] such a *labefactation* [decay] of all principles as may be injurious to morality."[23] But his position fluctuated somewhere between the extremes of Swift and Herring. Just before the oft-quoted sentence, Boswell has Johnson saying:

> As to this matter, which has been very much contested, I myself am of opinion, that more influence has been ascribed to "The Beggar's Opera," than it in reality ever had; for I do not believe that any man was ever made a rogue by being present at its representation. At the same time I do not deny that it may have some influence, by making the character of a rogue familiar, and in some degree pleasing.[24]

And Johnson followed his summary of Swift's and Herring's opinions with this:

> Both these decisions are exaggerated. The play, like many others, was plainly written only to divert, without any moral purpose, and is therefore not likely to do good; nor can it be conceived, without more speculation than life requires or admits, to be productive of much evil. Highwaymen and housebreakers seldom frequent the playhouse, or mingle in any elegant diversion; nor is it possible for any one to imagine that he may rob with safety, because he sees Macheath [the highwayman hero] reprieved on stage.[25]

Whatever the truth of the matter, *The Beggar's Opera* brought issues of the moral effect of art (specifically opera) and artists' moral responsibilities to the fore. Writing on all sides of the controversy proliferated. Boswell even planned to publish a collection of writings on the subject. We will return to it in relation to the famous statement attributed to Handel with regard to *Messiah:* "I should be sorry if I only entertained them, I wish to make them better." For now we only need to note the popularity of ballad operas, and in particular *The Beggar's Opera,* and the role they played in the downfall of Italian opera in England, and subsequently in turning Handel's career from opera to oratorio.

Handel and the Origin of Oratorio in England

Handel did not leave opera easily. After the Royal Academy's management of the King's Theatre was terminated in February 1729, he joined with a theater manager, John Jacob Heidegger, in the production of operas. They were given the use of the King's Theatre as well as the costumes, sets, and other assets of the Royal Academy for five years. During those years of the so-called Second Academy, Handel wrote eight new operas and repeated several of his previously composed operas, often with substantial revisions. But by 1734 this venture, too, had failed financially. So the early 1730s saw Handel turn his career a bit in the direction of oratorio, but hardly with the intent of abandoning opera.

In 1732 he resurrected one of his earlier works, the masque *Haman and Mordecai,* and revised it into *Esther,* his first English oratorio. He had composed and performed *Haman* sometime between the cessation of opera at the King's Theatre in the Haymarket in 1717 and the opening of the Royal Academy of Music in 1719. During that time he had also composed another masque, *Acis and Galatea,* his first extended dramatic work in English. Both works were probably performed at one of the residences of James Brydges, his patron at the time. The performances used chamber-sized musical forces, perhaps staged with some costuming and scenery.

After its original performance around 1718, *Haman and Mordecai* was not performed again until Handel's birthday, 23 February, in 1732. Renamed *Esther,* it was privately performed at the Crown and Anchor Tavern. The roles of the principal characters were played and sung by soloists who were joined by "a number of voices from the Choirs of the Chapel Royal and Westminster." The choirs were placed "after the manner of the Ancients . . . between the stage and the Orchestra." Handel attended the performance. So did Viscount Percival, who recounted in his diary, "From dinner I went to the Music Club, where the King's Chapel boys acted the *History of Hester.* . . . This oratoria or religious opera is exceeding fine, and the company were highly pleased, some of the parts being well performed."[27]

This production was repeated on 1 and 3 March. These three private performances led to a public performance in London on 20 April. That performance, evidently given without Handel's sanction, was based on a pirated copy of the score. Handel responded to the unauthorized performance by making a new, expanded version. It was advertised in the London *Daily Journal.*

By His MAJESTY'S *Command*

At the King's Theatre in the Hay-Market, on Tuesday the 2d Day of May, will be performed, *The Sacred Story* of Esther: an *Oratorio* in *English.* Formerly composed by Mr. *Handel,* and now revised by him, with several Additions, and to be performed by a great Number of the best Voices and Instruments.

N.B. There will be no Action on the Stage, but the House will
be fitted up in a decent Manner, for the Audience. The Musick is
to be disposed after the Manner of the Coronation Service.[28]

The "several Additions" were substantial. Handel expanded the
six scenes of the original masque to three acts, the standard operatic
length. This required eleven additional numbers. Six of them he newly
composed; the others he borrowed and reworked from some of his ex-
isting works. He also inserted two of the anthems he wrote for the coronation of King George II in 1727 — "My Heart Is Inditing" and
"Zadok the Priest." For this performance Handel used professional soloists from his opera company. The expansion resulted in a work that
was less integrated than the shorter original, but its combination of star
soloists from the Italian opera together with impressive choruses in the
style of English ceremonial anthems proved to be highly attractive. It
was "performed six times & very full."[29] Handel had hit upon a for-
mula that would prove to be perennially popular.

The note in the *Daily Journal* announcement about there being
"no Action on the Stage" is significant. Charles Burney, an eighteenth-
century music historian and chronicler, reported that "Dr. Gibson,
then bishop of London, would not grant permission for its being represented on that stage [in the Haymarket], even with books in the children's hands." He goes on to say that Handel then "had it performed at
that theatre . . . in *still life:* that is, without action, in the same manner
as Oratorios have been since constantly performed."[30] Were it not for
Bishop Gibson's prohibition to stage *Esther,* English oratorio might
have become a staged genre, and *Messiah,* with its unstageable libretto,
probably would not exist.

Esther was not the only non-staged dramatic English work Handel performed in 1732. On 15 May, less than two weeks after he performed his revised *Esther,* an unauthorized performance was given of
Acis and Galatea, the masque he had written about the same time as the
original *Esther.* Handel again responded with a revision and expansion
of the earlier version. In this case, the expansion consisted of arias from
one of the secular cantatas he had written during his Italian years, *Aci,
Galatea e Polifemo.*

Three of Handel's stars, Farinelli, Cuzzoni, and Senesino, appeared in a production of his opera, *Flavio*, c. 1728. Etching, English School (18th century).

That *Esther* and *Acis* achieved immediate popularity should come as no surprise. Richard Luckett has pointed out that by 1732 the English "were already thoroughly accustomed to long unstaged choral works, since these had for many years been a central feature of the annual celebrations for St. Cecilia's Day." This made the public "ripe for oratorio." The irony is that "the only person who seems not to have been was Handel himself."[31] He continued to try to keep Italian opera alive.

For the 1732-1733 season he wrote *Orlando*, one of his greatest operas; he also wrote a new oratorio, *Deborah*. But problems continued to mount. Handel's relationship with one of his star singers, Senesino, deteriorated to the point that the composer dismissed him. A competing opera company, the so-called Opera of the Nobility, formed for the next season. It successfully engaged Senesino, lured away most of Handel's other prized soloists, and took over the King's Theatre. Still Handel soldiered on with the performance of his operas, moving first to the theater at Covent Garden, and then, after the Opera of the Nobility's short life, back to the King's Theatre in 1738. Between late 1734 and spring of 1737 he composed six new operas.

In 1737 a burlesque opera satirizing Italian opera opened in the Little Theatre in the Haymarket, but it soon transferred to Covent Garden because it was so popular. That opera was *The Dragon of Wantley,* libretto by Henry Carey and music by John-Frederick Lampe. Carey, who listed himself on the title page as "*sig.* CARINI," was a poet and playwright best known, apart from *The Dragon,* for his poem "Sally in Our Alley." Like *The Beggar's Opera,* Carey's "Sally" was the basis for a twentieth-century musical, Jerome Kern's *Sally.* Lampe was a bassoonist in Handel's orchestra and a skillful composer. Carey's dedicatory letter to Lampe gives a good indication of the nature of their collaboration and the target of their satire — Italian opera.

To
Mr. *John-Frederick Lampe*

Dear Jack,

To whom should I dedicate this *Opera* but to You, for whose Interest it was calculated, and at whose Request it was completed: Many joyous Hours have we shared during its Composition, chopping and changing, lopping, eking out, and coining of Words, Syllables, and Jingle, to display in *English* the Beauty of Nonsense, so prevailing in the *Italian Operas.*

This Pleasure has been since transmitted to the gay, the good-natur'd, and jocular Part of Mankind, who have tasted the Joke and enjoy'd the Laugh; while the Morose, the Supercilious, and Asinine, have been fairly taken in, so far as to be downright angry; they say 'tis low, very low; now (begging their Worships Pardon) I affirm it to be sublime, very sublime. —

It is a Burlesque Opera:
And Burlesque cannot be too low.

Lowness (figuratively speaking) is the Sublimity of Burlesque: If so, *this Opera* is, consequently, the tip-top Sublime of its Kind. . . .[32]

The opera is set in the Yorkshire village of Wantley, a fictional name for Wharncliffe Cragge, near Sheffield, near which are a cave known as the Dragon's Den and a well called the Dragon's Well. A fire-breathing dragon threatens the lives of all in the area. His voracious appetite is described in the opening recitative and aria.

What wretched Havock does this Dragon make!
He sticks at nothing for his Belly's Sake:
He'll eat us all, if he 'bides here much longer!

AIR

Poor Children three,
Devoured he,
That could not with him grapple;
And at one sup,
He ate them up,
As one would eat an Apple.[33]

The hero is Moore of Moore-hall, a knight who loves the bottle and pretty lasses. He sings:

Zeno, Plato, Aristotle,
All were Lovers of the Bottle;
Poets, Painters and Musicians,
Churchmen, Lawyers and Physicians,
*   All admire a pretty Lass,*
*   All require a cheerful Glass.*
*   Ev'ry Pleasure has its Season,*
*   Love and Drinking are no Treason.*[34]

Margery, the daughter of Gaffer Gubbins, who is in love with Moore, begs him to go and slay the dragon. Moore acquiesces but with one requirement:

The only Bounty I require, is this,
That thou may'st fire me with an ardent Kiss;
That thy soft Hands may 'noint me over Night,
And dress me in the Morning e'er I fight.

Margery doesn't hesitate:

If that's all you ask,
    My Sweetest,
    My Featest,
    Compleatest,
    And Neatest,
I'm proud of my task.
Of Love take your fill,
    Past measure,
    My Treasure,
    Sole Spring of my Pleasure,
As long as you will.[35]

In the end Moore *"encounters the Dragon, and kills him by a kick on the Back-side."* Gubbins sings:

Most mighty *Moore,* what Wonders hast thou done?
Destroy'd the Dragon, and my *Marg'ry* won.
The Loves of this brave Knight, and my fair Daughter,
In *Roratorios* shall be sung hereafter.
Begin your Songs of Joy; begin, begin.
And rend the *Welkin* with harmonious Din.

and all join in chorus:

Sing, sing, and rorio,
An Oratorio
To gallant Morio,
    Of Moore-Hall . . .

CHORUS OF CHORUSES.

H U Z Z A ![36]

Like *The Beggar's Opera, The Dragon of Wantley* became tremendously popular. In fact, its initial run of sixty-nine performances outstripped *The Beggar's Opera*. It directly satirized Italian opera, and Lampe's music in Handelian style heightened the effect. As Carey put it in his dedicatory letter, "Your Musick . . . is as grand and pompous as possible, by which Means the *Contrast* is the stronger, and has succeeded accordingly."[37]

Though Handel complimented Lampe's music, he was still not fully ready to take the not-so-subtle hint of the last chorus, "Sing, sing and roroio/An oratorio." But during the late 1730s he gradually interspersed unstaged English works among his operatic productions. In addition to the aforementioned *Esther, Acis and Galatea,* and *Deborah,* these included the oratorios *Athalia* (1735), *Saul* (1739), and *Israel in Egypt* (1739) and the odes *Alexander's Feast* (1736), *Ode for St. Cecilia's Day* (1739), and *L'Allegro, il Penseroso ed il Moderato* (based on John Milton's poems *L'Allegro* and *Il Penseroso*) (1740). He also performed an extensive revision of his early Italian oratorio in 1737 and titled it *Il trionfo del Tempo e della Verità*. Finally, in January 1741, his career as an opera composer came to an end with *Imeneo* and *Deidamia*.

If changing from opera to oratorio was psychologically difficult for Handel, musically it was relatively simple. The subject matter was essentially the same in both genres. Like operas, oratorios typically told the exciting tales of ancient heroes, the only difference being that the heroes featured in oratorio came from the Old Testament and the Apocrypha instead of from secular ancient history. The English public readily identified with the heroes of the oratorios, especially since they were already in the habit of identifying God's favor toward ancient Israel with his supposed favor toward England.

Handel, by now a past master of the high Baroque dramatic style, easily transferred to oratorio the musical story-telling styles and techniques he had learned so well in writing opera. Just as in his operas, the story could be carried by his sure-handed recitatives, and the emotional responses of the characters to the dramatic situations could be captured in the vivid portrayal of affects in his arias.

One important ingredient of oratorio, however, did not come from opera — choruses. His operas made little or no use of choruses, but his oratorios gave the choir a substantial role. Fortunately, Handel possessed an exceptional talent for choral writing; it was perhaps even his greatest talent. Although before he started writing oratorios he had had relatively few occasions to exercise his choral writing skills, those occasions taught him how to make the magnificent choral climaxes that are so often the most thrilling moments in the oratorios.

All of the ingredients for success in this new venture were ready at hand — exciting, entertaining stories in English about the heroes of a divinely favored nation that was readily identified with England, and a composer with all the requisite skills to set those stories to music in a most compelling manner. Handel, shrewd businessman and entertainer that he was, recognized the potential for public success in these ingredients and spent the rest of his life concentrating on oratorio, leaving a legacy in that genre unmatched by any composer. After one more performance of an Italian opera, an unstaged version of *Imeneo* on 24 March 1742, Handel never returned to opera. The first performance of *Messiah* followed three weeks later, and a series of fourteen more oratorios followed during the next ten years, ending with *Jephtha* in 1752.

Chapter 3

Messiah

Messiah during Handel's Lifetime

Messiah, even apart from its unrivaled popularity, occupies a unique place among Handel's oratorios. Its text, unlike all the others except *Israel in Egypt*, comes exclusively from the Bible (often by way of the Book of Common Prayer), and it is not, in the usual sense, dramatic. It has no characters except for the angels in the Christmas scene and the crowd at the crucifixion, and it is largely not narrative (again in the usual sense). To some, that disqualifies it from being an oratorio. "Though that grand Musical entertainment is called an *Oratorio*," wrote John Brown in 1763, "yet it is not *dramatic;* but properly a Collection of *Hymns* or *Anthems* drawn from the sacred Scriptures."[1] The same notion prevails in Winton Dean's magisterial study *Handel's Dramatic Oratorios and Masques.* The book does not deal with *Messiah* because Dean does not classify it as a dramatic oratorio.

Certainly, these aspects set *Messiah* apart, but we will understand the work better if we recognize some fundamental similarities between *Messiah* and Handel's other oratorios. Like them, *Messiah* tells a hero story, albeit about an incomparably greater hero than any of the others. Its hero, though human like the others, is also divine, unlike the heroes of other oratorios, who are mere — and flawed — mortals. *Messiah* is not merely the story of a king or judge or general; it is the story of the King of Kings and Lord of Lords. Like other oratorios, *Messiah* offers drama, but whereas other oratorios present action that is limited in time and space, *Messiah* tells a cosmic drama that transcends both time and space. Although its plot contains minimal exterior action and few historical events, it is dramatic nonetheless. It is the incredible drama of humankind's deliverance from the tyranny of Satan, sin, and death by the long-promised Messiah. It unfolds in three "acts." The first focuses on the Messiah's birth, the second on his suffering, death, resurrection, and ascension. The third looks ahead to the resurrection of his saints and to his eternal reign. Charles Jennens, the compiler of the text, wrote that its subject "excells every other Subject." Therefore he hoped that Handel would "lay out his whole Genius & Skill upon it, that the Composition may excel all his former Compositions."[2]

Charles Jennens (1700-1773) was born into a wealthy family that had made its fortune in iron manufacturing. He inherited Gospal, the large family estate in Leicestershire, where he lived during the summer and fall months. But he moved to London during the winter and spring months for the concert season when, among other attractions, he could hear Handel. He was educated at Oxford as a classical scholar but received no degree because he would not make an oath of fidelity to King George I, Handel's former patron as Elector of Hanover, a Hanoverian usurper in Jennens's view. He became a notable Shakespeare scholar who planned a complete edition of Shakespeare's plays of which he completed five volumes before he died — *King Lear, Macbeth, Hamlet, Othello,* and *Julius Caesar.* George Steevens, another Shakespeare scholar, was jealous of Jennens and viciously disparaged Jennens's scholarly ability and character, a reputation that has lived on. One frequently quoted characterization of him has been attributed to Samuel Johnson:

> [Jennens is a] vain fool crazed by his wealth, who, were he in Heaven, would criticize the Lord Almighty; who lives surrounded by all the luxuries of an Eastern potentate — verily an English "Solyman the Magnificent"; who never walks abroad without a train of footmen at his heels, and . . . with a scented sponge 'neath his nose, lest the breath of the vulgar herd should contaminate his sacred person.[3]

Whoever gave this description, the derisive nickname "Solyman the Magnificent" comes to us from Steevens himself. So does Jennens's lasting reputation for vanity and scholarly incompetence. John Nichols printed a tirade by Steevens ("a gentleman who knew [Jennens] well"). And since "the attack, though severe, was on Vanity, not on Vice," Nichols did "not hesitate to retain the article."[4]

> In his youth he was so remarkable for the number of his servants, the splendour of his equipages, and the profusion of his table, that from this excess of pomp he acquired the title of *Solyman the Magnificent*. . . . The chief error of Mr. Jennens's life consisted in his perpetual association with a set of men every way inferior to himself. By these means he lost all opportunities of improvement, but gained what he preferred to the highest gratifications of wisdom — flattery in excess. . . .
>
> So enamoured . . . was our *Magnifico* of pomp, that if his transit were only from Great Ormond-street, Bloomsbury, where he resided, to Mr. Bowyer's, in Red Lion-passage, Fleet-street, he always travelled with four horses, and sometimes with as many servants behind his carriage. In his progress up the paved court, a footman usually preceded him, to kick oyster-shells and other impediments out of his way.

Steevens's rant was mostly given over to ridiculing Jennens's Shakespearian scholarship, which comes, he said, from one of those "who commence Authors in their dotage." Steevens also mentioned Jennens's authorship of *Messiah*, but disparaged it as "an easy task, as it is only a selection from Scripture verses."

Whatever Jennens's character faults may have been, they were balanced by admirable qualities. To his credit, Nichols reserved for himself "the right of subjoining . . . some proper antidotes." One anonymous correspondent praised Jennens's "charity and benevolence," which "was extensive, as that noble Religion, which he sincerely believed and practiced, prescribes. . . ." According to another correspondent:

> Mr. Jennens is a man of abilities; is conversant in the Polite Arts; that he understands Musick, Poetry, and Painting: I appeal to the Catalogue of his Pictures, which bear all the living testimony that

Pictures can bear of original and intrinsic merit. His taste in Musick is still less disputable — the compilation of the Messiah has been ever attributed to him. Handel generally consulted him; and to the time of his death lived with him in the strictest intimacy and regard. Respecting his knowledge in Poetry, the testimony of Mr. Holdsworth must principally be referred to.

This ingenious Author left to Mr. Jennens his most valuable Notes on Virgil, which were lately published, and received with the fullest approbation. Were Handel or Holdsworth men so mean or despicable, as to offer incense at the shrine of Ignorance?

Jennens was a devout Anglican. Ruth Smith, the leading scholar of Handel's English librettists, characterizes him as "a scholarly, evangelising supporter of the Church."

He left legacies for the Society for the Propagation of the Gospel in Foreign Parts and a fund for lectures on the catechism; he gave money for the rebuilding of the church in his family's parish of Nether Whitacre, and arranged for the parish tithes (which were due to him as landowner) to be returned to the church. He funded the publication of a treatise against atheism, his extensive library was stocked with hundreds of volumes of sermons and theological works, and his picture collection contained an unusually high proportion of religious, especially biblical, subjects.[5]

Modern scholarship has vindicated Jennens's scholarship. Shakespeare scholar Brian Vickers called him "an independent scholar of no mean ability" whose editions of Shakespeare were "vastly more scholarly than anything that had yet appeared."[6] We also know that Jennens was musically knowledgeable and had a deep admiration for Handel's music. Beginning in 1725, he subscribed to Handel's published works. Prior to supplying Handel with the *Messiah* libretto, he had provided him with the libretto of *Saul* and probably also of *Israel in Egypt*.

Handel was pleased to receive the *Messiah* libretto from Jennens, and when he began working on it on 22 August 1741, he worked very quickly. By 14 September he had finished the work. Such a pace was

Charles Jennens, who compiled the text for *Messiah,* said its subject "excells every other Subject." Portrait by Mason Chamberlain.

more or less typical for Handel. Romantic notions notwithstanding, it cannot be taken as a sign of exceptional or, as some have believed, divine inspiration. Like most of the composers of his time, Handel was capable of turning out a prodigious amount of music in a relatively short span of time. Upon completing *Messiah* he began to work almost immediately on *Samson,* a draft of which he finished on 29 October. He was following his normal work pattern of composing new works in the gap between concert seasons. He probably planned the two new oratorios for the upcoming 1741-1742 season at the King's Theatre. But somewhere along the way — the facts are largely unknown — he received and accepted an invitation to go to Dublin for that concert season.

Handel arrived in Dublin on 18 November, and on 29 December he wrote to Jennens, "It was with the greatest Pleasure I saw the Continuation of Your Kindness by the Lines You was [sic] pleased to send me, in Order to be prefix'd to Your Oratorio Messiah, which I set to Musick before I left England."[7] The lines Jennens sent Handel "to be prefix'd" to *Messiah* give its aim — MAJORA CANAMUS ("Let us sing of greater things") — and theme:

> And without Controversy, great is the Mystery of Godliness: God was manifested in the Flesh, justify'd by the Spirit, seen of Angels, preached among the Gentiles, believed on in the World, received up in Glory. In whom are hid all the Treasures of Wisdom and Knowledge.

Since he sent this prefatory material to Handel, Jennens must have expected him to perform *Messiah* while in Dublin, but he was less than pleased. He wrote to his friend Edward Holdsworth that "it was with some mortification to me to hear that instead of performing it here [in London] he has gone into Ireland with it. However, I hope we shall hear it when he comes back."[8]

In Dublin Handel arranged two series of subscription concerts. The concerts included performances of *L'Allegro, Acis and Galatea, Esther, Alexander's Feast,* and an unstaged version of his opera *Imeneo,* his final farewell to Italian opera.

The second series finished on 7 April 1742. Well before that time, plans were under way for the first performance of *Messiah*. According to an advertisement in the *Dublin Journal* of 27 March 1742, its performance would be "For Relief of the Prisoners in the several Gaols, and for the Support of Mercer's Hospital in Stephen's Street, and of the Charitable Infirmary on the Inns Quay."[9] On 10 April the same journal again announced the performance and requested "that the Ladies who honour this Performance with their Presence would be pleased to come without Hoops, as it will greatly encrease the Charity, by making Room for more company." A later announcement added that "The Gentlemen are desired to come without their Swords,"[10] again for the purpose of making more room to "encrease the Charity."

The first performance took place at the New Music Hall on Fishamble Street. It was a great success, as was the second performance on 3 June, the last concert of the season. Laudatory reviews ran in the *Dublin News Letter* and *The Dublin Journal*:[11]

[I]n the opinion of the best Judges, [*Messiah*] far surpasses anything of that Nature, which has been performed in this or any other Kingdom.

The Messiah . . . gave universal Satisfaction to all present; and was allowed by the greatest Judges to be the finest Composition of Musick that ever was heard. . . .

Words are wanting to express the exquisite Delight it afforded to the admiring crouded Audience. The Sublime, the Grand, and the Tender, adapted to the most elevated, majestick and moving Words, conspired to transport and charm the ravished Heart and Ear.

The Bishop of Elfin, Dr. Edward Synge, was in the audience. He, too, praised *Messiah* most highly.

As Mr. Handel in his oratorio's greatly excels all other Composers I am acquainted with, So in the famous one, called The Messiah he seems to have excell'd himself. The whole is beyond any thing I had a notion of. . . . It Seems to be a Species of Musick different from any other. . . . [T]ho' the Composition is very Masterly & artificial, yet the Harmony is So great and open, as to please all who have Ears & will hear, learned & unlearn'd.

Bishop Synge went on to attribute this greatness to Handel's "great care and exactness"; to the "Subject, which is the greatest and most interesting"; and to the "Words, which are all Sublime." He also added the following observation:

> And, to their great honour, tho' the young & and gay of both Sexes were present in great numbers, their behaviour was uniformly grave & decent, which Show'd that they were not only pleas'd but affected with the performance. Many, I hope, were instructed by it, and had proper Sentiments inspir'd in a Stronger Manner on their Minds.[12]

Controversy over Messiah

While oratorio in Germany was thought too sacred for performance in a theater and too theatrical for performance in a church (see chapter 1, p. 10), no trace of such a controversy arises in connection with *Messiah* performances in Dublin either in Bishop Synge's comments or in those of anyone else. But at the first performance in London the next year, the controversy came up again. Even before the first performance, it was criticized for desecrating the sacred story by being performed in a secular venue. An exchange that will amuse many of us today appeared in the daily papers. On 19 March 1743, a gentleman identifying himself as "Philalethes" wrote in the *Universal Spectator:*

> My . . . Purpose . . . is to consider, and, if possible, induce others to consider, the Impropriety of *Oratorios,* as they are now perform'd.
> Before I speak against them . . . it may not be improper to declare, that I am a profess'd Lover of *Musick,* and in particular all Mr. *Handel's Performances,* being *one* of the *few* who never deserted him. I am also a great Admirer of *Church Musick,* and think no

other equal to it, nor any Person so capable to compose it, as Mr. *Handel.* To return: An *Oratorio* either is an *Act* of *Religion,* or it is not; if it is, I ask if the *Playhouse* is a fit *Temple* to perform it in, or a Company of *Players* fit *Ministers* of *God's Word,* for in that Case such they are made.[13]

On 31 March 1743, another anonymous gentleman responded to Philalethes in the *Daily Advertiser* with the following verse:

Cease, Zealots, cease to blame these Heav'nly Lays,
For Seraphs fit to sing Messiah's Praise!
Nor, for your trivial Argument, assign,
"The Theatre not fit for Praise Divine."

These hallow'd Lays to Musick give new Grace,
To Virtue Awe, and sanctify the Place;
To Harmony, like his, Celestial Pow'r is giv'n,
T'exalt the Soul from Earth, and make, of Hell, a Heav'n.[14]

Philalethes could not let that go unchallenged, so he made a poem of his own which the *Universal Spectator* published on 16 April 1743. After some prose commentary on his verse, he concluded:

I must again assert [that theaters are] very *unfit* for *sacred Performances.* Nor can it be defended as *Decent,* to use the same Place one Week as a *Temple* to perform a *sacred Oratorio* in, and (when *sanctify'd* by those *hallow'd Lays*) the next as a Stage, to exhibit the *Bufooneries* of *Harlequin. . . .*[15]

Messiah was first performed in London on 23 March 1743; it was repeated two more times during that season. Though not unsuccessful, it certainly was not greeted with the warm enthusiasm that it had received in Dublin. The Earl of Shaftsbury recalled that *Samson* (performed in February) "was received with uncommon Applause" but *Messiah* was "indifferently relish'd." The cause was not only "the Scruples, some Persons had entertained, against carrying on such a Performance in a Play House," but also "for not entering into the genius of the Composition, this Capital Composition."[16]

Initially Jennens himself was not pleased. Even before hearing the oratorio, he voiced his dissatisfaction. "His Messiah has disappointed me," he wrote to Holdsworth, because Handel "set [it] in great haste, tho' he said he would be a year about it, & make it the best of all his Compositions."[17] He was less harsh after he heard it performed, though he still thought there was room for improvement. "'Tis after all, in the main, a fine Composition, notwithstanding some weak parts, which he was too idle & too obstinate to retouch, tho' I us'd great importunity to persuade him to it."[18] In 1745, Jennens again complained in a letter to an unknown recipient:

> I shall show you a collection I gave Handel, call'd Messiah, which I value highly, & he has made a fine Entertainment of it, tho' not near so good as he might & ought to have done. I have with great difficulty made him correct some of the grossest faults in the composition, but he retain'd his Overture obstinately, in which there are some passages far unworthy of Handel, but much more unworthy of the Messiah.[19]

The stress of the London concert season, along with the controversy surrounding *Messiah,* may have caused the return of Handel's "Paralytic Disorder, which affects his Head & Speech," as Jennens described the ailment.[20] (He had suffered from similar symptoms in the spring of 1737 after another particularly stressful period.) But by June he was well enough to return to composing. By September he had finished *Semele,* a work conceived as an English opera but performed as an oratorio, and *Joseph and His Brethren,* an oratorio. These were performed in February and March 1744, along with revivals of *Samson* and *Saul* — but no *Messiah.* Its first revival in London had to wait until the following year, when it was performed on Tuesday and Thursday of Holy Week. These performances took place in the King's Theatre in the Haymarket, apparently without public controversy about performing a sacred work in a theater. Then the next London performance was not until 1749 on Maundy Thursday in Covent Garden.

The Benefit Performance Tradition

Soon after this, Handel gave another concert in London. Though it was not a performance of *Messiah,* it had ramifications for *Messiah*'s future and long-term reception. The concert was a benefit for the Hospital for the Maintenance and Education of Exposed and Deserted young Children (Foundling Hospital). The 4 May 1749 minutes of the hospital's general committee read:

> Mr. Handel being present and having generously and charitably offered a performance of vocal and instrumental music to be held at this Hospital, and that the money arising therefrom should be applied to the finishing of the chapel of the Hospital.
>
> *Resolved* — That the thanks of this Committee be returned to Mr. Handel for this his generous and charitable offer.

The Foundling Hospital Chapel was the setting for numerous benefit performances of Handel's works, including *Messiah,* from 1749 to 1777. Hand-colored lithograph by M. & N. Hanhart from the engraving on stone by G. R. Sarjent (c. 1830).

Ordered — That the said performance be in the said Chapel on Wednesday, the 24th inst., at eleven in the forenoon.[21]

The concert took place at the unfinished chapel of the hospital, as ordered. It consisted of *Royal Fireworks, Anthem on the Peace,* selections from *Solomon* (relating to the dedication of the Temple), a concerto, and the *Foundling Hospital Anthem* ("Blessed are they that considereth the poor") which ends with the "Hallelujah Chorus" from *Messiah.* The concert was a great success. At least seven hundred people attended and a total of more than three hundred fifty pounds was raised for the hospital.

This concert was not the first benefit that Handel had produced. We have already noted that the first *Messiah* performance in 1742 was for the benefit of a hospital, prisoners, and other charities in Dublin. But Handel's charitable performances date farther back, at least to 1731, when he provided the music for a special service, the offering of which went to the Sons of the Clergy.

Then, in March 1739, Handel gave a concert that turned out to be the first in a series of benefits. It was announced in the *London Daily Post* on 20 March:

> For the Benefit and Increase of a Fund established for the Support of Decay'd Musicians or their Families. At the King's Theatre . . . this Day . . . will be reviv'd an Ode, call'd Alexander's Feast. Written by Mr. Dryden [music by Handel]. With several Concerto's on the Organ, and other Instruments. . . .[22]

Charles Burney noted the ability of music, especially Handel's, to raise money for charity.

> But the most honourable eulogium that can be bestowed on the power of Music is, that whenever the human heart is wished to expand in charity and beneficence, its aid is more frequently called in, than that of any other art or advocate. . . .
>
> Indeed Handel's Church-Music . . . has supported life in thousands, by its performance for charitable purposes: as at St. Paul's

for the Sons of the Clergy; at the Triennial Meetings of the Three Choirs of Worcester, Hereford, and Gloucester; at the two Universities of Oxford and Cambridge; at the Benefit Concerts for decayed Musicians and their Families; at the Foundling-Hospital; at St. Margaret's Church for the Westminster Infirmary; and for Hospitals and Infirmaries in general, throughout the kingdom, which have long been indebted to the art of Music, and to Handel's Works in particular, for their support.[23]

Messiah became the chief work used in charitable fund-raising. Burney remarked that "this great work has been heard in all parts of the kingdom with increasing reverence and delight; it has fed the hungry, clothed the naked, fostered the orphan, and enriched succeeding managers of the Oratorios, more than any single production in this or any country."[24]

In Handel's generous help for the poor, Marian Van Til sees him following in his father's footsteps. His father was a surgeon and a generous man "who clearly took to heart Jesus's teaching that 'to whom much is given, much will be required' (Luke 2:48)." He helped provide relief for plague victims in 1682, and throughout his career he "provided free medical care to those who couldn't pay for it." The sermon given at his funeral said that he was "calm and well meaning towards the poor and suffering [and] helped many through thick and thin by his skill and profession, even without payment." Van Til notes that this "surgeon's famous son would provide the equivalent of 'free medical care,' feeding and caring for Dublin's and London's orphans through benefit concerts of many of his music works, most notably *Messiah*."[25]

Although *Messiah* was not performed at the first Foundling Hospital benefit concert, it was performed at the next one in 1750, and then in annual benefit performances through 1777.

Handel's Final Years

Poor health and deteriorating eyesight prevented Handel from significant composing after 1752, when he completed *Jephtha*. In November 1752, he had an operation on his eyes, but its success was temporary.

The *London Evening Post* of 27 January 1753 said that "Mr. Handel has at length, unhappily, quite lost his sight."[26] In 1758, he may have been operated on by John Taylor, the same oculist who had operated unsuccessfully on Bach's eyes in 1750. A poem in the *London Chronicle* of 24 August bore the title "On the Recovery of the Sight of the Celebrated Mr. Handel, by the Chevalier Taylor," and a diary entry of 26 April mentions Handel in the company of "Taylor the occulist."[27] But if Taylor did operate on Handel's eyes, he was no more successful than he had been with Bach.

Handel was still able to plan a final series of concerts for March and April 1759: two performances of *Solomon,* one of *Susanna,* three of *Samson,* and two of *Judas Maccabeus.* The season ended with three performances of *Messiah,* the last that Handel would hear. According to Burney,

> The last Oratorio at which he attended, and performed, was on the 6th of April, and he expired on *Friday* the 13th, 1759, and *not on Saturday the 14th,* as was at first erroneously engraved on his Monument, and recorded in his Life; I have indisputable authority for the contrary: as Dr. Warren, who attended Handel in his last sickness, not only remembers his dying before midnight, on the 13th, but, that he was sensible of his approaching dissolution; and having been always impressed with a profound reverence for the doctrines and duties of the Christian religion, that he had most seriously and devoutly wished, for several days before his death, that he might breathe his last on *Good-Friday,* "in hopes, he said, of meeting his Good **God**, his sweet Lord and Saviour, on the day of his resurrection," meaning the third day, or the Easter Sunday following.[28]

Notwithstanding Burney's "indisputable authority," Handel died not on Good Friday; nor did he die on Thursday as five newspapers prematurely reported. Other newspapers, including at least one that had reported his death on Thursday, report that he died on Saturday the 14th. The last person to see Handel alive, other than his doctor, his apothecary, and a servant, was his friend James Smyth. On 17 April Smyth wrote to another of Handel's friend, Bernard Granville:

According to your request to me when you left London, that I would let you know when our good friend departed this life, *on Saturday last at 8 o'clock in the morn died the great and good Mr. Handel.* He was sensible to the last moment. . . . He took leave of all his friends on Friday morning, and desired to see nobody but the Doctor and Apothecary and myself. At 7 o'clock in the evening he took leave of me, and told me we "should meet again"; as soon as I was gone he told his servant *"not* to let me come to him any more, for that he had *now done with the world."* He died as he lived — a good *Christian,* with a true sense of his duty to God and man, and in perfect charity with all the world.[29]

The last codicil of his will, signed three days before his death, reads:

I hope to have the permission of the Dean and Chapter of Westminster to be buried in Westminster Abbey in a private manner at the discretion of my Executor, Mr. Amyand and I desire that my said Executor may have leave to erect a monument for me there and that any sum not Exceeding Six Hundred Pounds be expended for that purpose at the discretion of my said Executor.[30]

His funeral was anything but private. Some three thousand people attended, and the choirs of Westminster Abbey, St. Paul's Cathedral, and the Chapel Royal sang William Croft's *Burial Service.* He was buried in the poets' corner of the Abbey in accordance with the hope he expressed in his will. (One hundred ten years later, Charles Dickens would be buried at his feet.) Louis François Roubiliac, who made the monument of Handel for Vauxhall Gardens in 1738, also sculpted the monument that adorns Handel's grave. It includes a life-size image of Handel holding the music of one of the most-loved arias in *Messiah,* "I know that my Redeemer liveth."

Messiah after Handel's Death

Handel died, but *Messiah* lives on. Unlike all other music before it (except Gregorian chant, which is a special case, because it was preserved

GEORGE FREDERICK HANDEL. Efq.
born February XXIII. MDCLXXXIV.
died April XIV. MDCCLIX. *L.F.Roubiliac inv.^t et sc.^t*

The monument above Handel's grave in Westminster Abbey, London, England. Behind the statue of Handel is an organ with an angel playing a harp. On the left of the statue is a group of musical instruments and an open score of *Messiah,* and in front of him is the musical score of the aria "I know that my Redeemer liveth." Sculpture by Louis François Roubiliac, 1762. Photo by Eric de Maré.

by the Roman Catholic Church), *Messiah* never died. It marks the beginning of "classical" music in the sense that it has never had to be revived. As Richard Taruskin puts it: "The continuous performing tradition of European art (or literate) music . . . can . . . be said to begin with *Messiah,* the first 'classic' in our contemporary repertoire, and Handel is therefore the earliest of all 'perpetually-in-the-repertory' ('classical') composers."[31]

After the three London performances of *Messiah* in 1743, none were given there in 1744. But in 1744 it was performed in both Dublin and Cork, the Dublin performance being the start of an annual series there. In 1745, it was performed for the last time in the King's Theatre in the Haymarket, and then again in 1749 and 1750 in Covent Garden before beginning its series of annual performances at the Foundling Hospital. So, since its first performance in Dublin in 1742, there has been no year in which it hasn't been performed, and by 1750 annual performances of *Messiah* were already underway in Dublin and at the Foundling Hospital. During the 1750s it was performed in Salisbury, Oxford, Bristol, Bath, and Cambridge. It became a staple at the Three Choirs Festival, which began in 1757 and was held every year on a revolving schedule in Hereford, Gloucester, and Worcester.

Before the end of the century, it was being performed throughout the British Isles and had spread across the Channel, and even across the Atlantic. In Germany, Michael Arne conducted the first performance in Hamburg in 1772, and J. S. Bach's son Carl Philipp Emanuel conducted a performance in 1775. In Leipzig, in 1771, Johann Adam Hiller founded a singing school that began performing Handel oratorios in 1775. In 1786, he conducted the first performance of *Messiah* in Berlin (sung in Italian because he had only Italian singers available!). The first American performance occurred in 1770. It consisted of excerpts — the overture plus sixteen other pieces — performed in the Music Room in the New York City Tavern. During the 1770s, excerpts were also heard in Boston and Philadelphia. In 1817, the Handel and Haydn Society of Boston performed the three parts of *Messiah* over three nights (along with the three parts of Haydn's *Creation*). The following year they performed it complete in one night. Since 1854 they have been performing it annually, a record that surpasses even that of the famous Huddersfield Choral Society in England, whose annual performances of *Messiah* began in 1864.

Messiah also spread beyond the Western world. In fact, a more or less complete performance took place in India some three decades before the first American one. Its Indian performance resulted from the presence there of a popular English singer, Mrs. Cargill. Richard Luckett tells her intriguing story.

> Her father, a coal merchant, was so strongly opposed to her appearance as Polly in *The Beggar's Opera* at Covent Garden that he hired bruisers to abduct her; this was only thwarted when "the theatrical garrison sallied out in great numbers," Macheath's gang armed with their appropriate weapons. Her marriage to Mr. Cargill proving unsatisfactory, she bolted with an army officer to Calcutta, where she was an instant success in both *Messiah* and opera, cleared a great deal of money, but returning to England in the packet *Nancy,* was shipwrecked, and "found on the rocks of Scilly floating in her shift, an infant in her arms." She was under thirty.[32]

One of the correspondents whom John Nichols quoted in his *Literary Anecdotes,* published in 1812, wrote that the Jennens/Handel oratorios

> may have contributed more than any modern Sermons to Spread the knowledge of the finest and most interesting parts of Scripture, to which many besides the Great World might otherwise have paid little or no attention! We know not how widely the effects of *one* good action may extend. In some recent Voyage, I have read that Handel's Oratorios were favourite musick at the Philippine Islands.[33]

I cannot vouch for the accuracy of the writer's reporting, but if it wasn't accurate, it was at least prophetic.

Performing forces as a rule were not large in Handel's day, at least not by nineteenth-century standards. Handel's oratorios were not exceptions. Typically, an orchestra of about thirty-five and a choir of

View of the magnificent Box erected for their MAJESTIES, in Westminster Abbey under the Direction of Mr. JAMES WYATT, at the Commemoration of HANDEL.

Publish'd by J. Sewell 30 June 1784.

Messiah was performed by a chorus and orchestra of five hundred musicians in Westminster Abbey under the direction of James Wyatt at the first Commemoration of Handel on 30 June 1784. This illustration originally appeared in *European Magazine and London Review,* published by J. Sewell, in an article written by J. Dixon.

about twenty performed them. But in 1784, in commemoration (one year early) of the centennial of Handel's birth, an extravaganza of five concerts of Handel's music was given in Westminster Abbey and the Pantheon. *Messiah* was performed in Westminster Abbey at the third and fifth concerts. The orchestra and the chorus each included about two hundred fifty members. The Commemoration was repeated the following two years. In 1785 *The London Times* advertised that "The Band will be as numerous, and the Performances on the same Grand Scale" as the previous year. It also noted that "The Profits arising from the several performances, will be applied to the FUND for *Decayed Musicians, the Westminster Hospital, and St George's Hospital.*"[34] The tradition of performing Handel's music for the benefit of charities continued, and the tradition of gargantuan performances had begun. After a gap, another Commemoration took place in 1791, and the great composer Joseph Haydn attended. Another attendee described the scene:

> On entering the Abbey I was filled with surprise at the magnitude of the orchestra; it rose nearly to the top of the west window and above the arches of the main aisle. On each side there was a tier of projecting galleries and I was placed in one of these. Above us were the trumpeters and appended to their instruments were richly embossed banners worked in silver and gold. We had flags of the same description which gave the whole a gorgeous and magnificent appearance. The arrangement of the performers was admirable, particularly that of the sopranos. The young ladies were placed upon a framework in the center of the band in the form of a pyramid, as you see flowerpots set up for a show. This greatly improved the musical effect. The band was a thousand strong, ably conducted by Joah Bates upon the organ. . . . Haydn was present at this performance and with the aid of a telescope, which had been placed on a stand near the kettledrums, I saw the composer near the king's box.[35]

While in London, Haydn heard more performances of Handel's music, which greatly inspired him. "He is the father of us all," Haydn exclaimed to Giuseppe Carpani, one of his early biographers. Carpani added that Haydn said "that when he heard Handel's music in London, he was so struck by it that he began his studies all over again as if he had known nothing until that time. He mused over every note and extracted from these learned scores the essence of real musical magnificence."[36]

The monumental Westminster Abbey concerts marked the beginning of a trend that continued through the nineteenth century and well into the twentieth. We can see the extremes to which that trend went in the statistics of some of the performances. In 1857, a chorus of more than six hundred voices sang *Messiah* in a performance by the Boston Handel and Haydn Society. But even that was modest compared to what happened at the Crystal Palace. In 1857, in a "Trial Festival" for the upcoming centennial celebration, *Messiah* was performed with about two thousand singers and five hundred instrumentalists. Then, to commemorate the centennial of Handel's death in 1859, the Grand Handel Commemoration Festival mustered a chorus of 2,765 members and an orchestra of 460. If the *Guinness Book of World Records* has a category "biggest *Messiah* performance — excerpts only," his entry is probably the ten thousand voices and five hundred instruments that performed the "Hallelujah Chorus" at the National Peace Jubilee in Boston in 1869.

It seems that for a time, this expansion knew no limits. In 1843, a writer in the *Musical Examiner* asked:

> Who ever heard of a choir too large for Handel? Here the physical capacity of the ear is the only limit to the desires of the mind. Not though nations should be formed into choirs, and the genius of thunder were to swell the harmony till it shook the very spheres, would the true votary of Handel cry "Hold, enough!"[37]

Some "true votaries of Handel" did cry enough! One of them was the playwright and music critic George Bernard Shaw, who wrote,

> In England [Handel's] music is murdered by the tradition of the big chorus! People think that four thousand singers must be four thousand times as impressive as one. This is a mistake: they are not even louder. . . . You can get a tremendously powerful *fortissimo*

The five-hundred-voice Calvin College Augmented Chorus of Grand Rapids, Michigan, pictured here in a 1933 performance at the new Civic Auditorium, reflected the trend that continued into the mid-twentieth century of performing *Messiah* with large chorus and orchestra.

from twenty good singers . . . because you can get twenty people into what for practical purposes is the same spot; but all the efforts of the conductors to get a *fortissimo* from the four thousand Handel Festival choristers are in vain: they occupy too large a space; and even when the conductor succeeds in making them sing a note simultaneously, no person can hear them simultaneously, because sound takes an appreciable time to travel along the battle front four thousand strong. . . .[38]

And in another context, Shaw wrote,

We know rather less about [Handel] in England than they do in the Andaman Islands, since the Andamans are only unconscious of him, whereas we are misconscious. To hear a thousand respectable young English persons jogging through *For He shall purify the sons of Levi* as if every group of semiquavers [sixteenth notes] were a whole bar of four crotchets [quarter notes] a capella, or repeating *Let Him deliver Him if He delight in Him* with the same subdued and uncovered air as in *For with His stripes we are healed,* or lumbering along with *Hallelujah* as if it were a superior sort of family coach: all this is ludicrous enough; but when the nation proceeds to brag of these unwieldy choral impostures, these attempts to make the brute force of a thousand throats do what can only be done by artistic insight and skill, then I really lose patience.[39]

Sheer size was not the only way and, except for the grotesque extremes, not the most serious way in which posterity tampered with Handel. As tastes changed during the late eighteenth and nineteenth centuries, re-orchestrators "improved" the few older works that survived in the performed repertory, *Messiah* being chief among them, by bringing them into line with more "advanced," contemporary standards. People arrogantly and patronizingly thought that anachronistic performance practices improved on an "old master."

Modernized orchestrations of *Messiah* were common. Mozart was the first and certainly most distinguished re-orchestrator of *Messiah*. He turned Handel's Baroque orchestra into a Classical one. In *Messiah,* in addition to the strings, Handel only called for two oboes, two trumpets, and tympani. Mozart added pairs of flutes (and a piccolo in the *pifa*), clarinets, horns, bassoons, and three trombones.

Subsequent orchestrators added more anachronistic instruments — including harp, tuba, cymbals, and other percussion — making the orchestra into a Romantic one. Sometimes orchestrators justified this practice by referring to the speed with which Handel composed *Messiah*. He wrote, so the Romantic story goes, at such a feverish pace, in the heat of such extraordinary inspiration, that he could not have bothered with petty details like orchestration. But, as noted earlier, Handel's speed of composition was not extraordinary, either by his own standards or by those of most of his contemporaries. Certainly nothing is careless or incomplete about his orchestration of *Messiah*. It is typical high Baroque orchestration done with the excellence that nobody should have doubted from a composer as gifted as Handel.

Monumental size and Romantic "improvements" of *Messiah* went hand in hand with a changed conception of its nature. It became less and less an "elegant entertainment" of the eighteenth century and more and more a sacrosanct musical icon of the nineteenth — in other words, a typical example of art as religion (as opposed to art in the service of religion), and of a religion of feeling (as opposed to a religion of the Word). "Handel is not a mere composer in England," Shaw tartly commented. "[H]e is an institution. What is more, he is a sacred institution. When his Messiah is performed, the audience stands up, as if in church, while the Hallelujah chorus is being sung. It is the nearest sensation to the elevation of the Host known to English Protestants."[40]

"Why . . . does not somebody set up a thoroughly rehearsed and exhaustively studied performance of The Messiah," Shaw asked, "with a chorus of twenty capable artists? Most of us would be glad to hear the work seriously performed once before we die."[41] Shaw was born too soon; were he alive now, he would find plenty of performances to satisfy him. Today many performers strive to turn gargantuan *Messiah* back into Handel's *Messiah*. They scale down the choir and orchestra to Handelian size, retain Handel's orchestration, and use eighteenth-century instruments or replicas of them. By playing on eighteenth-century instruments and mastering their capabilities, by studying the musical treatises of the time, and in general by approaching the music from its historical sources and context, these performers have learned much about Baroque articulation, phrasing, rhythm, tempo, ornamentation — in short, about all those elements that influence the vitality and expressiveness of a performance. The results have been a revelation and have proved, if any proof was needed, that Handel did indeed know what he was doing.

Now historical consciousness affects most *Messiah* performances. Although many still use large numbers of performers, few rely on anachronistic orchestrations, and many apply styles of performance learned from the more intentionally historically conscious performers.

Of course, the tradition of performing *Messiah* with large choirs that grew out of late eighteenth- and nineteenth-century ideals has an authenticity of its own, and the artistic result is still a very good piece of music. Handel's choral style can withstand substantial increases in number far more successfully than those of his greatest contemporary, J. S. Bach, whose intricate and highly detailed counterpoint gets hopelessly blurred by too large a choir. Furthermore, performing *Messiah* with large choirs gives many more people the wonderful experience of participating in the performance of this great music — no small consideration!

By the late twentieth century, gargantuan choruses and orchestras performing *Messiah* had given way to more modestly sized ensembles, and their performance style reflected historical consciousness. The Calvin College Oratorio Society, pictured here in 2006, is among them.

Purpose

"I wish to make them better"

George Frideric Handel, 1733. Oil on canvas by Balthasar Denner (1685-1749). Deutsches Historisches Museum, Berlin, Germany.

Chapter 4

To Teach and Delight

When *Esther*, Handel's first English oratorio, was performed in May 1732, members of the royal family attended all four of its performances. The *Daily Courant* reported, "His Royal Highness the Prince of Wales, and the Three Eldest Princesses, went to the Opera-House in the Hay-Market, and saw an Entertainment call'd ESTHER, an *Oratorio*, in English."[1] When *Messiah* was first performed in Dublin, the *Dublin News-letter* referred to it as an "elegant Entertainment."[2] Jennens himself referred to it as "a fine Entertainment."[3] Commenting on the *Daily Courant* report, Howard Smither made the point that oratorios were meant to be entertainment.

> Significant in this report, and in others like it, is the word *entertainment*, for Handel's performances of *Esther* in the opera house established the English oratorio as a musico-dramatic entertainment without staging. Despite its sacred subject, the English oratorio was not intended primarily to be a vehicle of devotion; it was a concert genre more closely related to the theater than the church.[4]

Smither didn't go so far as to eliminate a devotional purpose, but he definitely tilted the balance on the side of entertainment: oratorio "was not intended primarily to be a vehicle of devotion" and it was "more closely related to the theater." By contrast, Jens Peter Larsen put the theater and the church on equal footing when he said: "Oratorio acknowledges two masters, the church and the theatre."[5] In view of the

Handel's first English oratorio, *Esther*, was staged in London at the Crown and Anchor tavern, shown in this 1851 watercolor, as well as at the London Opera House.
Drawing on paper by J. Findlay, 1851, the British Museum.

sacrosanct status that accrued to *Messiah* during the nineteenth century and continued throughout much of the twentieth — and is still alive today — the role of entertainment needs to be emphasized if the balance is to be righted.

That emphasis might not sit well with some who love *Messiah* and its message deeply. They might point to the well-known anecdote in which Lord Kinnoull paid Handel a compliment on the fine entertainment *Messiah* had provided the audience. Handel is reported to have replied, "I should be sorry if I only entertained them, I wish to make them better."[6]

We don't know whether Handel actually made that statement. Philosophy professor James Beattie relates the anecdote in a letter to a Rev. Dr. Laing dated 25 May 1780, a little more than twenty years after Handel's death. Beattie told Laing that he had "lately heard two anecdotes" from Lord Kinnoull, "with whom [Handel] was particularly acquainted."[7] The first anecdote is about the audience (including the king) standing when the choir sang, "For the Lord God Omnipotent reigneth." The second contains the remark that concerns us here. (I'll refer to it as "Handel's" remark. It is certainly a remark he could have made, but putting his name in quotation marks indicates the attribution is questionable.)

"Handel's" remark does not invalidate Smither's contention that oratorios were meant to entertain. It does not reject entertainment as a goal. It rejects it as the *only* goal: "I should be sorry if I *only* entertained them." That concession, however, will probably not satisfy those who balk at the notion that Handel's oratorios, especially *Messiah*, are entertainment at all. The reason they are not ready to accept *Messiah* as entertainment, I think, is that today the meaning of the word has sunk to a lowest-common-denominator level, a level suggested by words like "amusement" and "diversion" — the level Samuel Johnson had in mind when he said of *The Beggar's Opera*, "The play, like many others, was plainly written only to divert, without any moral purpose."[8]

During the eighteenth century the word "entertainment" had not yet come to be used only for amusements that were merely titillating, mindless, and "without moral purpose." Not all entertainments were meant "only to divert." Entertaining pastimes could be noble, wholesome, and intellectually stimulating — even spiritually instructive and edifying. In fact, such entertainment was considered a special domain of the arts. According to an ancient theory of art that was still alive in Handel's time (though being strongly challenged), the purpose of art was to offer such entertainment. The theory maintained that the purpose of art is "to teach and delight" — the teaching being not of information but, as the Renaissance poet Sir Philip Sydney put it, of "moral doctrine, the chief of all knowledges."[9] "Handel's" remark falls right in line with that strand of thought. "I should be sorry if I only entertained [delighted] them, I wish to make them [teach or inspire them to be] better."

Entertaining people and making them better were not seen as incompatible goals. To teach — ethics and morality, not mere facts and information — and to delight were seen as two complementary poles around which art revolved. Of course, the emphasis changed from time to time. For example, although the ancient poet Horace wrote that the poet's aim is "to blend in one the delightful and the useful," literary critic M. H. Abrams points out that Horace "held pleasure to be the chief purpose of poetry, for he recommends the profitable merely as a means to give pleasure to the elders, who, in contrast to the young aristocrats, 'rail at what contains no serviceable lesson.'"[10] But if Horace put greater weight on pleasing, others at different times and places put greater weight on teaching. For theorists who viewed art as non-trivial — as something that mattered in life — teaching was the ultimate end, delighting or moving were proximate ends. That was definitely the case during the Renaissance and the ensuing Baroque period. For Sydney

> Poetry, by definition, has a purpose — to achieve certain effects in an audience. It imitates only as a means to the proximate end of pleasing, and pleases, it turns out, only as a means to the ultimate end of teaching; for "right poets" are those who "imitate both to delight and teach, and delight to move men to take that goodnes in hande, which without delight they would flye as from a stranger. . . ."[11]

A generation after Sydney, another poet, Ben Jonson, articulated the same theory. Of course a poet must have "elocution, or an excellent faculty in verse" in order to attract and delight, but Jonson stressed that the poet must also have "exact knowledge of all virtues, and their contraries; with ability to render the one loved, the other hated, by his proper embattling them."[12] More expansively, in his Dedication to *Volpone*, Jonson wrote:

> For, if Men will impartially, and not a-squint, look toward the Offices and Function of a Poet, they will easily conclude to themselves the Impossibility of any Man's being the good Poet, without first being a good Man. He that is said to be able to inform young Men to all good Disciplines, inflame grown Men to all great Virtues, keep old Men in their best and supream State, or, as they decline to Childhood, recover them to their first Strength; that come forth the Interpreter and Arbiter of Nature, a Teacher of Things divine, no less than human, a Master in Manners, and can alone (or with a few) effect the Business of Mankind. . . .[13]

Lest the foregoing examples seem chronologically removed from Handel and irrelevant with regard to music, allow me one more quotation, this from Johann Mattheson, a musician and theorist whom Handel knew from his time in Hamburg. According to Mattheson, a musician's task is "to present the virtues and vices in his music well, and to arouse skillfully in the feelings of the listener a love for the former and a disgust for the latter. *For it is in the true nature of music that it is above all a teacher of propriety.*"[14] Mattheson required of the musician the qualities attributed to poet Sir Thomas Wyatt (d. 1542):

> A visage stern and mild, both did grow
> Vice to contemn, in virtue to rejoice.[15]

The view that the goal of art is to delight and teach (with teaching being the ultimate end) was alive in Handel's time but was being supplanted by theories of art that either eliminated its teaching function or at least made delight the ultimate end. Charles Burney defined music as "the art of pleasing" and "an innocent luxury, unnecessary, indeed, to our existence."[16] Given this shift in aesthetic theory that was taking place, Beattie's anecdote containing "Handel's" remark can be seen as an attempt to affirm the older emphasis by enlisting the authority of Handel. "Handel's" remark fits well with Beattie's position regarding the relationship of teaching and pleasure in art. Normally, the relationship was seen as "delighting in order to teach" — art as the sugar-coating, as it were, on the bitter pill of moral rectitude. The poet, as Sydney put it, "doth not only show the way, but giveth so sweet a prospect into the way, as will entice man to enter into it."[17] But Beattie gave it a different slant. He wrote that, whereas historians and philosophers "please that they may instruct," poets "instruct that they may the more effectually please."

> Pleasing, though uninstructive, poetry may gratify a light mind; and what tends even to corrupt the heart may gratify profligates: but the true poet addresses his work, not to the giddy, nor to the worthless, nor to any party, but to mankind; and, if he means to please the *general* taste, must often employ instruction as one of the arts that minister to this kind of pleasure.[18]

However the relationship was viewed, teaching and delighting were not seen as incompatible, and neither one was seen as detrimental or inimical to art. They belonged together. But just as that mutuality bothers some because they think of entertainment only in terms of its lowest common denominator, so it bothers others who have too exalted a view of art, thinking that it has no ulterior aim ("art for art's sake"), and that it sullies itself when it stoops to "moralize." For them art has nothing to do with morality and should be exempt from moral or ethical criticism. Due to the influence of the Enlightenment, that idea was gaining credence in Handel's time, and it is still with us today. As art critic Roger Kimball points out, "We suffer from a peculiar form of moral anesthesia, an anesthesia based on the delusion that by calling something 'art' we thereby purchase for it a blanket exemption from moral criticism — as if being art automatically rendered all moral considerations beside the point. . . ."[19] From the perspective of history, however, the view that art is amoral is the peculiar one. The normal view, taken by most people in most times and places, sees art as being closely related to ethics and morality. And even in our own society, where moral criticism is much frowned upon, literary critic Wayne Booth has noticed that no one seems to resist it for long.

> Even those critics who work hard to purge themselves of all but the most abstract formal interests turn out to have an ethical program in mind — a belief that a given way of reading, or a given kind of genuine literature, is what will do us most good.[20]

Beattie, Mattheson, and others believed that the artist should produce works that, while pleasing, "will do us most good." Upon hearing *Messiah*, Bishop Synge said, "Many, I hope, were instructed by it, and had proper Sentiments impres'd in a Stronger manner on their minds."[21] Jennens and Handel, no doubt, held the same hope.

Chapter 5

Messiah versus Deism

"If the powerful stories we tell each other really matter . . . then criticism that takes their 'mattering' seriously cannot be ignored."[1] And if critics must take stories' "mattering" seriously, so, of course, must the tellers.

Handel was a story-teller. He devoted the biggest part of his professional life to telling stories. His musical story-telling was first done principally through his operas and later through his oratorios, opera's sacred counterpart. The specific operatic tradition out of which Handel's operas and oratorios both grew was the tradition of *opera seria*, a tradition that took story-telling seriously. Not all operatic traditions did. Almost from the beginning, as Richard Taruskin notes, the world of opera was "a divided world, its two political strains — the edifying and the profitable, the authoritarian and the anarchic, the affirmational and the oppositional — unpeacefully coexisting, the tension between them conditioning everything about the genre. . . ."[2] *Opera seria* fell on the edifying, authoritarian, affirmational side of the divide. Its librettos were

> vehicles for noble sentiment — noble in both the literal and the figurative sense of the word. Real tragedy . . . was deemed unsuitable for moral instruction. . . . A happy ending . . . was mandatory in an opera libretto even if it contradicted historical fact; for as Marita McClymonds, a leading historian of "reform" opera, has observed, "poets were expected to portray what, according to an orderly moral system, should have happened rather than what actually did happen."[3]

In a word, the plots of *opera seria* were "moralizing." For example (and overly simplified), Handel's *Rodelinda* taught faithfulness and *Admeto* taught self-sacrifice. Handel, like other composers of *opera seria*, followed Mattheson's dictate that a musician's task was "to present the virtues and vices in his music well, and to arouse skillfully in the feelings of the listener a love for the former and a disgust for the latter."

But Handel also entertained. His operas, in their dual function of teaching and pleasing, exemplify the time-honored aesthetic theory discussed in the previous chapter. Or to use Taruskin's terminology, his operas were both "edifying and profitable" (at least until they became financially unprofitable) and the coexistence of these qualities in his works was not "unpeaceful." Unquestionably, Handel was a man of the theater with a keen business sense. He most certainly aimed to please; his financial success depended on it. But he also aimed to teach; that is what made his art "matter." So when *opera seria* no longer proved financially viable, he did not take the next easiest road to financial success — the road that was already paved by *The Beggar's Opera*. Instead, he blazed a new trail.

The new trail, English oratorio, nevertheless had much in common with the old *opera seria* road. Handel's English oratorio, no less than *opera seria*, entertained. His music gave soloists ample opportunity to showcase their virtuosity and the beauty of their voices, and to that attraction Handel added the splendor of the choruses. As one of Handel's librettists put it, "the Solemnity of Church-Musick is agreeably united with the most pleasing Airs of the Stage."[4] Oratorios, like operas, also featured entertaining stories. Their sacred source notwithstanding, their stories sometimes contained the perennial attractions of sex and violence — and if they were missing from the original, they might be added. But they were also more than entertaining stories. Again, like opera, they told stories that provided moral teaching. Much of what oratorios taught was similar to what operas taught — love of virtue and hatred of vice. For example, in *Saul* Handel leads us to admire Jonathan's loyalty and to abhor Saul's pride and jealousy. But teaching by means of sacred stories in oratorio could be more explicitly Christian than in opera. *Theodora* (Handel's favorite, and his only oratorio based on a saint's life) teaches faithfulness, chastity, and self-sacrifice — virtues that also might be promoted in opera — but with distinctive Christian coloring.

English oratorio, like *opera seria,* required a happy ending. Handel's *Jephtha* offers an interesting example. Unlike Carissimi's *Jephte* which follows the reading of most Bible translations and ends tragically, Handel's *Jephtha* has a happy ending. Instead of Jephtha's daughter being sacrificed as a burnt offering, an angel appears, calls a halt, and explains that "No vow can disannul / The law of God" — that is, the law that forbids child sacrifice. Instead, Iphis (Jephtha's daughter's name in the oratorio) is devoted to God in perpetual virginity. But this ending was not, as it might seem, a willful rewriting of the biblical account simply to achieve a happy ending. As Ruth Smith points out, it stemmed from an English translation of the biblical text that many commentators of the time accepted. Thomas Morell, the librettist, was following Samuel Humphreys (another of Handel's librettists), who translated the crucial sentence, "Whatsoever cometh forth of the doors of my house to meet me . . . shall surely be the Lord's, or [*not* 'and'] I will offer it up as a burnt offering." In this translation, then, Jephtha's vow is that he "will sacrifice what first encounters him, *or* devote it to God; and so his daughter is devoted to God, in the sense of perpetual virginity."[5] In the oratorio, Morell rendered Jephtha's vow precisely according to Humphreys' translation:

> What, or who-er shall first salute mine Eyes,
> Shall be for ever thine, or fall a sacrifice.

In the most common type of happy ending in Handel's oratorios, Israel receives deliverance from its enemies. *Israel in Egypt, Esther, Deborah, Judas Maccabeus,* and *Joshua* are obvious examples. *Samson,* too, ends happily. Even though the hero dies, his death brings deliverance from the Philistines. The oratorios that take their names from evil leaders, whether from within Israel (for example, *Athalia*) or from outside (for instance, *Balshazzar*), also end in deliverance: Athalia is dethroned and Joash takes her place; Balshazzar is defeated by Cyrus, who then frees Israel from captivity. Such oratorios, of course, exemplify various heroic virtues similar to those found in the heroes of the operas. But the oratorios' stories are not ultimately about the deliverance of a nation from its enemies by a great hero. The heroes were God's instruments; deliverance ultimately came from God. So the oratorios end with choruses of praise and thanksgiving to God. And since eighteenth-century English Christians, like the Israelites, worshipped the God of Abraham, Isaac, and Jacob, the stories of Israel's deliverance served to revive their hope and strengthen their courage. Regrettably, those Christians tended to read the stories in narrowly political and nationalistic ways, identifying God's favor toward Israel with his favor toward England. But beyond their chauvinistic readings, they could legitimately take the stories of deliverance as types of God's deliverance of his people from bondage to sin and death.

Messiah also tells a deliverance story — the story of God's ultimate deliverance of his people from bondage to sin and death. But it is a story that increasing numbers of Europeans were disbelieving, and therein lies the motivation behind Jennens's compilation of the Scripture passages that constitute the libretto for *Messiah*.

The Enlightenment was in full swing, and the church was severely threatened by those who denied that Christ was the Son of God, the long-promised Messiah who would deliver his people from bondage to sin and death. Of course the church had always faced threats to the faith from unbelievers. But the number of unbelievers in Europe increased significantly during the Enlightenment, a movement that fostered "natural" religion that proclaimed a commonsense social morality and an optimistic view of human nature. Typically it took the form of Deism. Deism did not deny the existence of a Supreme Being who created all things but claimed that after creation that Being left humans to themselves. According to Deists, humans had no need of a god because they were innately good and had the resources to solve their own problems. Human perfectibility could be achieved by human resources without divine intervention. Thus Deism was fundamentally at odds with Christian beliefs that humans are basically sinful, that they are incapable of saving themselves, and therefore that they need a Savior. In other words, Deists did not believe in the need for a Messiah.

Messiah was born into this world of growing Deistic threat to the church. It was not only that Deism added substantially to the number of Europeans who didn't believe Jesus to be the Messiah, but also that unlike other disbelievers (Jews, Muslims, atheists), Deists were often within the church, even among the clergy — "profane scoffers among our selves," as Richard Kidder called them.[6] Committed orthodox Christians like Jennens had reason to be concerned, and that concern spawned an outpouring of works that reaffirmed the historic Christian beliefs, the chief among them being that Jesus Christ is the Son of God, the Messiah. Jennens's libretto for *Messiah* joined a host of writings on the subject. Treatises and tracts, poems and periodical articles were written to prove that Jesus was the Messiah prophesied in the Old Testament. And of course many sermons were preached on the subject. The famous Boyle Lectures, instituted in the will of the great chemist Robert Boyle (d. 1691), "required the annual lecturer to give eight sermons 'proving the Christian Religion against notorious Infidels, viz. Atheists, Deists, Jews and Mahometans,' and by 1737 an abridged version of them filled four volumes."[7]

One of the more prominent defenders of the Christian faith was the aforementioned Richard Kidder. Between 1684 and 1700, he published three volumes titled *A Demonstration of the Messias*. He included some of the content from his Boyle Lectures of 1693 and 1694. A second edition of all three parts was published in 1726. Jennens had a copy in his library, and its list of contents, as Ruth Smith writes, "reads like a blueprint for the libretto of *Messiah*."[8]

The subtitle of Kidder's book reads: *in which the truth of the Christian Religion is proved especially against the Jews.* His controversy with the Jews is both apologetic and evangelical. In his preface he wrote that the book "is a defence of our common Christianity."[9] And he ended Part III with these words: "And may the same GOD take away the *veil* that is upon the hearts of the *Jews,* that they may be converted and saved!"[10]

The 1726 edition of Kidder's *Demonstration* extended the subtitle to include "all the enemies" of the Christian religion. It seems likely that the addition to the subtitle was made in response to the growing threat of Deism. And indeed Kidder claimed in the preface that his arguments would be a "great force against the Deists."[11] But Kidder's method of argumentation from Old Testament prophecy, fitting though it be when addressed to Jews and Christians, seems an unlikely way to convince Deists, who were skeptical about anything that couldn't be proved by "natural religion." But it would be wrong to assume that Kidder's (and Jennens's and others') argumentation from Old Testament prophecy could be used only to convert Jews and strengthen the faith of Christians, and not also to convince Deists, counter-intuitive though it might seem. Christian writers were beginning to realize that trying to argue for their faith on the basis of narrowly rationalistic and naturalistic assumptions was ceding too much territory to the Deists. So instead of trying to prove Christianity by using only the purely rationalistic methods the Deists accepted, thus removing the possibility of mystery, they began to admit boldly that much about Christianity indeed is mysterious, "in defiance," as Ruth Smith puts it, "of the first major deist salvo, [John] Toland's *Christianity not Mysterious.*"[12] In this light, we can see that Jennens's use of Old Testament prophecy was not only for the conversion of Jews and the nurture of Christians; it also aimed at persuading Deists.

In a letter to Holdsworth, Jennens wrote: "Our Maker has a right to speak to us in what Language he pleases, & to humble our Pride with things above our Understandings."[13] In the recitative that precedes "The trumpet shall sound," the bass soloist sings, "Behold, I tell you a mystery." But the mystery he tells, the resurrection of the dead, incredible as it is, is not the only mystery proclaimed in *Messiah.* Indeed it is all mystery; it is all "above our Understandings." Jennens proclaimed that fact in the motto for *Messiah* he sent to Handel in Dublin: "Great is the mystery of Godliness."

In compiling the libretto of *Messiah,* Jennens was joining the chorus of pamphleteers, poets, preachers, and authors of large theological tomes in defending the orthodox Christian faith. He was fully aware of the threat of Deism. He saw its eroding effect on the church all around him. That in itself could account for his vigorous defense of orthodox Christianity. But an event close to home must have reinforced his fears and redoubled his efforts. As Smith tells it, when Jennens was twenty-eight years old,

> his younger brother Robert, who had followed the family tradition of studying first at Oxford and then at the Inns of Court, cut his

throat and threw himself out of the window of his rooms in Middle Temple. To Jennens, a devout Christian, this must have been more than the death of his brother by a sudden and horrible end; religion taught that in dying by his own hand Robert had committed an irreparable sin and lost the hope of salvation. Most agonizing of all, as it transpired, he had died a victim of that religious radicalism which churchmen of the time so feared. In the investigations following his death, he was found to be in correspondence with another Oxford graduate, a professed deist who gloated to Robert about the converts to scepticism he had made. Robert was judged from this exchange of letters to have been preyed upon by doubt and (perhaps sharing his elder brother's tendency to depression), rather than becoming aggressively heretical like his correspondent, to have despaired and taken his own life.[14]

It is not fanciful to suggest that Jennens was still haunted by his brother's suicide when, a decade or so later, he began to work on the *Messiah* libretto. He probably had hopes of converting "Atheists, Deists, Jews and Mahometans" and anyone else who did not believe Jesus Christ to be the Messiah, but he may have been more concerned to stem the tide of Deism by preventing or dispelling doubts and despair like those that played a role in his brother's tragic end. In any case, he certainly was heavily invested in the project. Whether it was to convert unbelievers or to strengthen and encourage believers, his choices of Scripture passages were masterfully made. No wonder he submitted the text to Handel, the composer most qualified to add the rhetorical force and splendor of music to the sublime texts he had chosen; no wonder he expected Handel to put forth his very best effort; and then no wonder he was disappointed to learn that Handel had spent only three weeks composing the music. But he need not have worried. History has more than vindicated his choice of Handel. Jennens could have had no idea that Handel's music would carry the story of *Messiah* around the world, uninterrupted to this day.

Commentary

"Great is the mystery of Godliness"

George Frederick Handel. Portrait by Thomas Hudson
(1701-1779), from a private collection.

Chapter 6

Before We Begin

Some General Musical Considerations

Since oratorio is a close relative of opera, an understanding of some of the conventions of opera presents a good starting point for understanding oratorio.

One aspect of Handel's operatic language is his choice of genre. Opera in Handel's time consisted mainly of two genres of solo singing, recitative and aria. Recitative, as its name implies, is recitation-like. In it the voice declaims a text without repetition of words (except occasionally for rhetorical emphasis) and usually with just one note for each syllable of text. The rhythms of the music, with rhetorical exaggeration, follow the rhythm of the words, and the melodic contours, again with rhetorical exaggeration, follow the inflections of speech. Because in recitative the declamation of the words is of highest importance, accompaniment is minimal so as not to obscure the words. Often it consists only of basso continuo accompaniment (such as cello and harpsichord), in which case it is called *secco* recitative. In opera, *secco* recitative typically carries the dialogue and the dramatic action of the story.

The other type of vocal solo, the aria, moves away from declamation to lyricism and often to virtuosity. Aria repeats words and phrases of text frequently and uses rhythms that tend away from the irregularity of speech to the regularity of bodily (dance) rhythms. Often, several (sometimes very many) notes accompany one syllable of text. Such passages are called melismas. Instruments play a greater role in aria than in recitative, often being equal partners with the voice. In opera an aria typically "portrays" the principal emotion (or affect, in eighteenth-century terminology) that has been generated by the action and dialogue of the preceding recitative. So Baroque opera consists largely of segments in which the drama unfolds in recitative followed by moments during which action is suspended while one of the characters sings an aria portraying the principal affect generated during the preceding recitative. The result is sometimes called "opera of affects" because periodically the dramatic action is interrupted while an aria portrays an affect for the audience's contemplation.

Between the two extremes of recitative and aria there are two subtypes of recitative. One, accompanied recitative, uses other instruments of the orchestra in addition to the basso continuo. Accompanied recitative usually portrays the more dramatic moments in the narrative or dialogue. The other subtype, arioso, leans in the direction of aria by being less speech-like and more song-like. It was typically used for the more lyrical moments in the narrative or dialogue.

Handel inherited these types of solo vocal music from opera when he turned to writing oratorios, and since he spent so much of his career composing operas, by the time he turned to oratorio he was a past master of them all. But oratorio featured another genre, an extremely important one, that was almost entirely lacking in opera — the chorus. Before turning to oratorio, Handel had little opportunity to gain experience in this area. He did, however, have a few occasions to write choral music — some Latin church music and two Italian oratorios while he was in Italy, the Brockes Passion, occasional English anthems, and a few non-staged dramatic works in English. But though his experience was relatively limited, his talent wasn't. Composing choral music seems to have been a natural talent for him.

Messiah presented a problem, however, in using recitative and aria. All of the words come from the Bible. Isaiah and the other biblical writers were not, of course, thinking of the recitative/aria format of Baroque opera, and Jennens did not rewrite the biblical story in new literary styles that lent themselves to being set as recitatives and arias. More specifically, with a few brief exceptions, no characters in the story speak any of the words. So even though Jennens's collection of texts

has a narrative aspect, no obvious division between narrative and response presents itself.

Handel found a simple and effective solution. In his basic
scheme, he took each unit of text, each "scene," and set it in a progres-
sive order beginning with recitative and then moving through aria to
chorus. The cumulative effect of such a sequence is not only musically
effective, but it also underscores the climax toward which the texts typically progress. Furthermore, arias and choruses generate a sense of response even when the text continues to be narrative; listeners sense
emotional response at the same time as the narration continues.

Throughout Part I of *Messiah*, Handel maintained this pattern
with minor exceptions. Parts II and III are much less regular. In the
following commentary, we will consider reasons for the exceptions as
they occur.

A second aspect of Handel's musical language is well-known because it is one of the easiest things to point out about the way he set
words to music. He made abundant use of a technique known as
"madrigalism," so called because it first flourished in the madrigals of
the Renaissance. Madrigalism refers to imitation of a word or phrase
by the music — for example, an ascending scale on the word "climb,"
fast notes on "run," a sharp dissonance on "pain," and the like. Handel
hardly ever passed up an opportunity to use madrigalisms, and he was
especially imaginative in inventing them. Something about this may
seem a bit naïve, however. Further, music doesn't have to resort to such
obvious bits of imitation to express a text effectively; any two-bit composer can do it. But if composers as great as Josquin and Lassus,
Monteverdi and Schütz, Bach and Handel, and Beethoven and
Brahms used such seemingly naïve tricks, perhaps we should think
twice before dismissing their importance for effective text-expression.
But even granting the importance (though not the necessity) of
madrigalisms for text-expression, they are hardly the only, or even the
main, expressive "tool" a composer has. If they were, musical expression would be severely limited. After all, how many words or phrases
can be literally illustrated in music?

Madrigalism can best be thought of as one of many rhetorical devices. That is how Baroque music theorists categorized them. They

considered madrigalisms to be analogous to illustrations in verbal rhetoric. And just as verbal rhetoric consists of many more devices than illustration, so too musical rhetoric consists of many more devices than madrigalism. Anything a composer does that is out of the ordinary serves as a rhetorical device: getting louder or softer; speeding up or slowing down; pausing; taking a peculiar melodic turn or harmonic direction; leaving a dissonance unresolved; doing something unexpected with the form or using an unusual combination of instruments — anything, in a word, that calls attention to a word or phrase or idea in the text.

Finally, Handel had at his disposal a "vocabulary" of musical conventions that provided a common ground of understanding between composer and audience. Certain musical styles, gestures, techniques, and instruments had "meaning" that both composer and listener understood. The composer did not aim to create a highly individualized and original expressive language. Rather, the composer attempted to use commonly understood rhetorical devices and "vocabulary" as vividly and imaginatively as possible.

Mottoes

After Handel had gone to Dublin, Jennens sent him mottoes for the title page of *Messiah*. Jennens was fond of supplying mottoes. In a letter to his friend Holdsworth, he wrote that "many of our best authors make use of them." He confesses, "whenever I scribble to the publick, I cannot resist the Temptation of adorning my Title page with any significant motto that comes into my head & seems a propos."[1] The two he sent to Handel for *Messiah* are certainly apropos.

The first is a mere two-word Latin phrase from Virgil's Fourth Eclogue: *majora canamus* ("Let us sing of greater things"). Handel had been singing of great things throughout his professional life in his operas about the great deeds of the heroes of ancient history. He continued to sing of the great deeds of heroes when he turned to oratorio, only the heroes came from ancient Hebrew history. Now Jennens enlisted Handel's prodigious talent to sing of someone far greater than any ancient hero, namely the Messiah, the King of Kings and Lord of Lords.

Notably, Christians had long thought that Virgil's Fourth Eclogue, from which Jennens took the motto, contained a prophecy of Christ's birth in the lines:

> Jam redit et Virgo, redeunt Saturnia regna,
> Jam nova progenies caelo dimittitur alto. . . .

> Now returns the Virgin, returns the reign of Saturn;
> now a new generation is sent down from high heaven. . . .

The poet Alexander Pope (1688-1744) found Virgil's lines so concordant with Isaiah that he rendered Virgil's supposed prophetic lines as follows:

> Rapt into future times, the Bard begun:
> A Virgin shall conceive, a Virgin bear a Son!
> From Jesse's root behold a branch arise,
> Whose sacred flow'r with fragrance fills the skies.[2]

Following the Latin heading, Jennens added two verses from Paul's epistles: "And without controversy, great is the Mystery of Godliness: God was manifested in the flesh, justified by the Spirit, seen of angels, preached among the gentiles, believed on in the world, received up in glory [1 Tim. 3:16]. In whom are hid all the treasures of wisdom and knowledge [Col. 2:3]." The whole story of *Messiah* is summed up in those verses. According to Henry Hammond (1605-1660), in a book that Jennens probably knew,[3] "manifested in the flesh" refers to "the several articles of our faith from the Birth to the Assumption [ascension] of *Christ*"[4] — covered in *Messiah* numbers 2-33. The rest of *Messiah* covers further details that Hammond outlined in his paraphrase of the verse from Timothy:

> He was beheld and confess'd and adored by Angels themselves . . .
> he was . . . preached and proclaimed not only to the Jews, but

Gentiles . . . he was received and believed on by many of all nations through the world; and . . . he was visibly and with a glorious appearance of Angels taken up into heaven, there to reign for ever in the glory of God the Father. . . .[5]

Chapter 7

Part the First

The Coming of the Messiah

1. *Orchestra:* Sinfony

SCENE 1

2. *Arioso:* Comfort ye, comfort ye my people
   Accompanied recitative: The voice of him that crieth in the wilderness
3. *Aria:* Every valley shall be exalted
4. *Chorus:* And the glory of the Lord shall be revealed

SCENE 2

5. *Accompanied recitative:* Thus saith the Lord
6. *Aria:* But who may abide the day of His coming
7. *Chorus:* And He shall purify the sons of Levi

SCENE 3

8. Secco *recitative:* Behold, a virgin shall conceive
9. *Aria and chorus:* O thou that tellest good tidings to Zion
10. *Accompanied recitative:* For behold, darkness shall cover the earth
11. *Aria:* The people that walked in darkness have seen a great light
12. *Chorus:* For unto us a Child is born

SCENE 4

13. *Orchestra:* Pifa
14. Secco *recitative:* There were shepherds abiding in the field
    Accompanied recitative: And lo, an angel of the Lord came upon them
15. Secco *recitative:* And the angel said unto them
16. *Accompanied recitative:* And suddenly there was with the angel
17. Turba *chorus:* Glory to God in the highest

SCENE 5

18. *Aria:* Rejoice greatly, O daughter of Zion
19. Secco *recitative:* Then shall the eyes of the blind be opened
20. *Aria:* He shall feed His flock like a shepherd
21. *Chorus:* His yoke is easy

1. *Orchestra:* Sinfony

The overture to *Messiah* (called a "sinfony" by Handel) provides an excellent example of a Baroque musical convention that conveyed a specific meaning to its listeners. This type of overture, which originated in French opera, consists of two sections. The first part is slow and pervaded by dotted rhythms, that is, a long note followed by a short note (or group of notes), the long note being at least three times the length of the short one. The stately movement of the dotted rhythms suggested royal pomp and splendor, in particular the entrance of King Louis XIV. The second section is fast and probably owes its origin to a long-standing courtly practice in which a lively dance follows a stately. By Handel's time (and even long after), the French overture, or more specifically the stately dotted rhythms that characterize the first section, "meant" solemn ceremony and royal splendor. Other aspects of the music — harmonies, melodic gestures, and so on — could tilt this affect in various directions so that, for example, it could be celebrative for a royal victory or dirge-like on the occasion of a royal death. But whatever the more specific affect, the French overture would have immediately suggested to Handel's audiences the pomp and ceremony associated with royalty. Although Handel usually began an oratorio with a French overture, here, for an oratorio about the King of Kings, doing so is particularly appropriate.

Did Handel wish it to suggest something specific about the King at this point? I think not. Although a certain severity and perhaps even a hint of elegy shade the first section and a note of joyful exultation colors the second section, this overture gives a rather general affect. Had Handel tipped the affective character of the overture too far in one direction or another, he would have weakened the impact of the succeeding numbers. The overture alerts the audience that a serious matter is at hand and suggests the coming of a king. But the kind of king and what his arrival portends are unclear, especially since the exuberance of the fast section is tempered by its minor key and by the final cadence that returns to the severity of the opening section.

Scene 1

2. *Arioso:* Comfort ye, comfort ye my people, saith your God; speak ye comfortably to Jerusalem, and cry unto her, that her warfare is accomplished, that her iniquity is pardoned.

   Accompanied recitative: The voice of him that crieth in the wilderness: Prepare ye the way of the Lord, make straight in the desert a highway for our God.

3. *Aria:* Every valley shall be exalted, and every mountain and hill made low: the crooked straight and the rough places plain.

4. *Chorus:* And the glory of the Lord shall be revealed, and all flesh shall see it together: for the mouth of the Lord hath spoken it (Isa. 40:1-5).

After the somewhat severe ending of the overture we hear something very different. E minor is gone. The strings of the orchestra play quietly pulsing, smoothly connected chords in E major. In order to achieve the desired effect, the bows caress the strings almost as a mother would caress her distraught child. The gently stroked E major chords immediately suggest tenderness. Before a word is sung, the orchestra "speaks" of comfort.

After the orchestra's introduction, the tenor soloist sings "Comfort ye" — three notes gently descending by step, long-short-long. Nothing could be simpler or more direct. The orchestra immediately echoes the tenor. More elaborate and extended statements follow — "Comfort ye my people" — adding rhetorical emphases, while the orchestra accompanies with gently stroked chords as in the introduction. At the end of each phrase of text the orchestra echoes the simple three-note "comfort ye" motive.

A change occurs as the tenor identifies the source of the comforting message: "saith your God." The orchestra momentarily drops out, allowing the words to come through without obstruction. They are sung to the three-note "comfort ye" motive, but with two alterations that change its character from tender to strong. The motive ascends rather than descends, and instead of the long-short-long (trochaic) rhythm, it has three equal notes (spondaic). For further emphasis they are repeated at a higher pitch. At the end of the phrase the orchestra repeats the original form of the motive, thus adding "comfort ye" to the tenor's "saith your God."

Tenor: "saith your God,"   "saith your God."
Orchestra: ["comfort ye"]   ["comfort ye"]

The orchestra introduces the next section by resuming the gently stroked chords. After a measure and a half the tenor continues the comforting message in a longer phrase: "Speak ye comfortably to Jerusalem." The longer phrase obviously requires new music to accommodate its length, but the three-note "comfort ye" motive is not abandoned. It appears as the cadence notes at the end of the phrase — "[Je]-ru-sa-lem." The phrase recurs more intensely a step higher and leads to a climax that emphasizes the change in verb from "speak" to "cry." The tenor's voice jumps up an octave and sings the phrase without any accompaniment: "and cry unto her." Cry what? The gently stroked chords resume in the orchestra as the tenor tells us "that her warfare is accomplish'd, that her iniquity is pardon'd." "Her warfare" is repeated in another rising sequence that culminates and cadences, appropriately, on "accomplish'd." But the peak of intensity of the whole section arrives on the word "iniquity," sung to a high, dissonant note, which lasts a whole measure before it is resolved on "pardon'd." The release of the tension on "pardon'd" after the long-held dissonance on "iniquity" offers a perfect musical analogue to the forgiveness of sin.

With the source and the content of the comforting message announced, the text and the musical style change. A voice "in the wilderness" cries out, "Prepare ye the way of the Lord, make straight in the desert a highway for our God." At the literal level, as Roger Bullard points out, the "wilderness" that Isaiah was envisioning was the desert

> from Babylonia, the land of exile, to Israel, the once more Promised Land. Ordinarily the traveler going from Babylonia to Israel would follow the curvature of the Fertile Crescent, avoiding the desert; but this road is to cut directly through the arid wilderness. It is the Lord who will be traveling that road, leading his people homeward.[1]

The Gospels identify the voice as John the Baptist's (Matt. 3:1-3, Mark 1:1-3, Luke 1:17, and John 1:23), so as we hear the tenor singing Isaiah's words we also hear John the Baptist bidding his listeners to "prepare the way of the Lord . . . a highway for our God." For this injunction Handel changed from the lyrical arioso style of "Comfort ye" to a dramatic, declamatory accompanied recitative with strong punctuating chords in the orchestra.

In the aria that follows, the text tells what will happen when the Lord God comes: "Every valley shall be exalted, and every mountain and hill made low: the crooked straight and the rough places plain." Metaphorically, the desert between Babylon and the Promised Land represents this sin- and strife-filled world. The imagery of its valleys being exalted and its mountains and hills being brought low resonates with words from the Magnificat of the Virgin Mary: "He hath put down the mighty from their seats, and exalted them of low degree" (Luke 1:52).

The text is full of contrasts — exalted and low, crooked and straight, rough and plain — that provided Handel with abundant opportunities for madrigalisms, opportunities that he obviously relished!

All this leads to the climactic chorus: "And the glory of the Lord shall be revealed." The text features four components. Handel gave each its own characteristic musical gesture and combined them in a variety of ways within the overall framework of a lively dance. The phrase "And the glory of the Lord" is always sung to a rising line that reaches its peak on "Lord." "Shall be revealed" always descends, suggesting the incarnation. (See Example 1 below.)

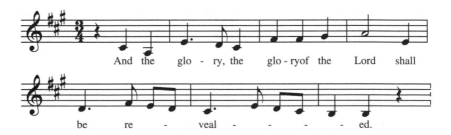

EXAMPLE 1

"And all flesh shall see it together" is suggestive of a down-to-earth, rustic dance; its music is simple, repetitive, and rhythmically infectious. The fourth phrase, "for the mouth of the Lord hath spoken it," stands out from the rest. To suggest the rock-solid certainty of God's word, Handel set the phrase to long, strong, repeated notes. It is sung only by the outer voices, framing the music from top to bottom. (See Example 2 on p. 93.)

Scene 2

5. *Accompanied recitative:* Thus saith the Lord of Hosts: Yet once a little while, and I will shake the heavens and the earth, the sea and the dry land, and I will shake all nations, and the desire of all nations shall come (Hag. 2:6-7). The Lord whom ye seek, shall suddenly come to His temple, even the messenger of the cov-

EXAMPLE 2

enant, whom ye delight in, behold, He shall come, saith the Lord of Hosts.

6. *Aria:* But who may abide the day of His coming? And who shall stand when He appeareth? For He is like a refiner's fire.

7. *Chorus:* And He shall purify the sons of Levi, that they may offer unto the Lord an offering in righteousness (Mal. 3:1-3).

Donald Burrows observed that "In Part One, accompanied recitatives are used when the prophet (metaphorically) raises his voice."[2] We noticed that in the first scene at "The voice of him that crieth in the wilderness." It happens again at the beginning of Scene 2, when the prophet thunders, "Thus saith the Lord of Hosts," and then gives a message that stands in stark contrast to the comforting and joyous message of Scene 1. Apparently there is more to the story than comfort and joy. Scene 2 looks at the Lord's coming from a different point of view, one that is at first terrifying rather than comforting.

The orchestra introduces the opening recitative with a dotted rhythm reminiscent of the overture, but now the rhythm is much quicker and sounds menacing. The words proclaim a warning: "Yet once a little while, and I will shake the heavens and the earth, the sea and the dry land, and I will shake all nations."

Along with the dotted rhythms in the orchestra, the most prominent musical feature of the recitative is the long runs of fast sixteenth notes, sung by the bass, that emphasize (and, with a little imagination, illustrate) the frightening word "shake." Beginning at the words "all nations I'll shake," the orchestra leaves its dotted rhythms for rapidly repeated sixteenth notes, a style known in the Baroque period as *stile concitato,* the "agitated" or "warlike" style. Then, at "and the desire of all nations shall come," the bass sings the same run of sixteenth notes he sang on "shake," but now the notes are ascending instead of descending, and at the same time the orchestra changes from its *stile concitato* sixteenth notes to legato eighth notes reminiscent of the accompaniment of "Comfort ye." These changes were prompted, not accidentally, by the word "desire." They give the music an ironic tone similar to Amos taunting the people for expecting the Day of the Lord, the day of God's victory over his enemies, hardly counting on the possibility that when that day should come, the Lord might count his own people among his enemies:

Alas for you who desire the day of the Lord!
　Why do you want the day of the Lord?
It is darkness, not light;
　　as if someone fled from a lion,
　　and was met by a bear. (Amos 5:18-19)[3]

In response to the frightening recitative, the aria follows with a timorous question sung to a plaintive melody in D minor: "But who may abide the day of his coming?" And if the reason for fear was not sufficiently clear in the recitative, the aria adds another: "For He is like a refiner's fire." In its original form the aria was for a bass soloist, and the music did not have much contrast between the two sections of text. Except for some melismas on "fire," the "refiner's fire" music was similar to the music of "But who may abide." It was all in the same slow, plaintive style. Not until 1750 did Handel rewrite the aria in the form that is now familiar — an alto aria with two vividly contrasting sections.

Handel made the change to take advantage of the availability of a particular singer. The biggest singing stars of the time were castrati, men who had been castrated as boys to preserve their soprano or alto vocal range. In 1750, a famous alto castrato, Guatano Guadagni, came to England with an Italian troupe of comic singers. He became all the rage in London for his virtuosity and showmanship. Handel eagerly added Guadagni to his company and gave him the alto solos in *Samson* and *Messiah* that spring. (Handel also composed the alto solos in *Theodora* specifically for him.) Guadagni's presence prompted Handel to make substantial revisions in "But who may abide." Of course, he changed it from bass to alto range, and he made some relatively small revisions for the first section. But the big change was in the "refiner's fire" section, for which he wrote entirely new music. The vocal part takes full advantage of Guadagni's virtuosity, and the strings play feverishly fast repeated notes — marked *prestissimo,* Handel's fastest tempo marking — which occasionally dart upward like flames. It is a *stile concitato aria* taken to the limit. In one stroke Handel provided Guadagni with a "show-stopper" and portrayed the flames of the refiner's fire much more vividly.

Frightening as this scene has been to this point, in the end there is still comfort, but comfort not without pain. The fire is a refiner's fire. Its heat is real and intense, but its end is purification of "the sons of Levi." As Matthew Henry explains, the sons of Levi are

> all those that are devoted to his [Christ's] Praise, and employ'd in his Service, as the Tribe of *Levi*, was, and whom he designs to make *unto our God* spiritual *Priests*, Rev. 1.6. a *holy Priesthood*, 1. Pet. 2.5. *Note*, All true Christians are *Sons of Levi*; set apart for God to do the Service of his Sanctuary, and to *War the good Warfare*.[4]

Although the music is still in a minor key, it is a lower, more relaxed key (the subdominant key, for those who know music theory). It starts with the same plaintive descending interval that began "But who may abide," but now the tempo is faster and the accompaniment lighter. And although the tempo is faster than "But who may abide," it is considerably slower than the "refiner's fire" music that immediately precedes it. All in all its music strikes the right balance. It is serious enough to keep the shaking and the burning in mind, but joyous and light enough to convey the outcome which, though painful, is purification.

Handel derived the music of the chorus from one of his other works, a secular Italian cantata for two voices and continuo. Despite turning the duet into a four-part chorus with orchestra, he managed to retain its light, airy texture. Most of the time, the orchestra is only minimally involved or simply doubles the voices. All four voice parts seldom sing together; in fact, even three voice parts rarely sing together. The solo and duet textures of the cantata predominate. Only for the last phrase of text do the voices all come together, bringing to God "an offering in righteousness."

Scene 3, section 1

8. Secco *recitative:* Behold, a virgin shall conceive, and bear a son, and shall call His name Emmanuel, God with us (Isa. 7:14, Matt. 1:23).

9. *Aria and chorus:* O thou that tellest good tidings to Zion, get thee up into the high mountain; O thou that tellest good tidings to Jerusalem, lift up thy voice with strength; lift it up, be not afraid; say unto the cities of Judah: Behold your God (Isa. 40:9)! Arise, shine, for thy light is come, and the glory of the Lord is risen upon thee (Isa. 60:1).

Scene 3 continues the same kind of "light/dark" alternation that Handel set up in Scenes 1 and 2. In the first section of Scene 3 we hear the good tidings that "light is come"; a virgin shall bear a son. It opens with a recitative in D major following the G minor ending of Scene 2. Unlike the recitatives in the previous scenes, this one is *secco*, accompanied only by the harpsichord and cello. The simple, natural declamation of the voice matches its minimal accompaniment. The great mystery of the virgin birth is appropriately announced with little fuss. As Roger Bullard puts it: "The virgin birth is a mystery. Not a riddle or puzzle for which we can find some explanation, but a mystery, before which we can only come in the kind of awe communicated by the alto's soft assurance that in this mystery, God is with us."[5] Those final words, "God with us," are subtly highlighted by a pause after "Emmanuel." The pause, though brief, is just enough longer than the previous ones to heighten an attentive listener's expectation for what follows: "God with us."

In response to the alto's announcement comes a call to proclaim the good news: "O thou that tellest good tidings to Zion . . . say unto the cities of Judah: Behold your God . . . thy light is come, and the glory of the Lord is risen upon thee." In issuing this call the aria continues the narrative, while at the same time it expresses the joy generated by the news it brings. It is exuberant, dance-like, and filled with upward leaps and melodic sequences that illustrate its words: "get thee up into the high mountain," "lift up thy voice," "arise," "the glory of the Lord is risen upon thee." Its music makes connections with earlier pieces. It begins with the same interval as the aria ("But who may abide") and chorus ("And he shall purify") of Scene 2. In fact, the first several notes of all three pieces are remarkably similar in melodic shape, which connects the three texts, while the rhythmic and harmonic differences highlight the progression from one to another — from the plaintive "But who may abide" (D minor, slow) through the tempered joy of "And he shall purify" (G minor, moderately fast) to the uninhibited joy of "O thou that tellest good tidings" (D major, fast). Another musical feature relates "O thou that tellest good tidings" to Scene 1. In two places — at "get thee up into the high mountain" and "say unto the cities of Judah" — the music has the same rhythm as "and all flesh shall see it together" from the chorus "And the glory of the Lord."

The sequence of movements in the previous two scenes leads us to expect a chorus to follow the aria, but Handel has a surprise for us. Although he does give us a climactic chorus, it comes in an unexpected way. Just when the alto soloist leads into what would normally be the orchestral conclusion of the aria, the choir breaks in and develops the anticipated conclusion into a full-fledged chorus. The fusion of a chorus to the end of the aria efficiently brings this section of the scene to its climax, a climax that is all the more effective because the choir provided Handel additional musical resources to highlight the climactic words "Behold your God" and "the glory of the Lord is risen upon thee."

Scene 3, section 2

10. *Accompanied recitative:* For behold, darkness shall cover the earth, and gross darkness the people: but the Lord shall arise upon thee, and His glory shall be seen upon thee. And the Gentiles shall come to thy light, and kings to the brightness of thy rising (Isa. 60:2-3).

11. *Aria:* The people that walked in darkness have seen a great light, and they that dwell in the land of the shadow of death, upon them hath the light shined (Isa. 9:2).

12. *Chorus:* For unto us a child is born, unto us a Son is given, and the government shall be upon His shoulder, and His name shall be called Wonderful, Counsellor, the mighty God, the everlasting Father, the Prince of Peace (Isa. 9:6).

The perspective shifts again. A virgin, we've heard, will bear a son who will be "God with us." That promise is so sure that the messengers can shout to Zion, in the present tense, that "the glory of the Lord is risen upon thee." But the promise has yet to be fulfilled, and the text shifts again to the dark side. The second section of Scene 3 speaks of darkness that covers the earth and of the people wandering aimlessly in that darkness. But the situation changes from dark to light more quickly here than in Scene 2. There the good news of purification was not heard until the chorus at the end, after both the recitative and aria had warned us of the frightening aspect of the Messiah's coming. Here in Scene 3, section 2, the dark gives way to the light in both the recitative and the aria, and then the light shines fully throughout the final chorus.

Handel's masterful tone-painting vividly captures in sound the contrast between light and dark. The recitative, in arioso style, is divided into two sections. The first, "For behold, darkness shall cover the earth," portrays darkness with low range, a minor key, dissonant harmony, and ominously rustling sixteenth notes in the strings. When the voice completes the words "and gross darkness the people," the music is poised for a cadence in B minor. But instead it jumps without preparation into the bright key of D major as the voice begins the next phrase of text, "but the Lord shall arise upon thee." The strings cease their sixteenth-note rustling, the harmonies become consonant, and the range, now higher, keeps rising. The strings remain in the higher part of the range as the bass soloist sings "and his glory shall be seen upon thee." The harmonies modulate to a still brighter key, A major, and by the end of the final phrase, "the brightness of thy rising," the first violins have climbed back to the highest note of the piece, and the music has cadenced on a bright F♯ major chord. Light has driven out the darkness.

The subject and the imagery of the following aria are the same as in the recitative — darkness giving way to light — and Handel's music makes the contrast between darkness and light as vivid as he did in the recitative. But the aria's text adds another element. It focuses on the people trapped in the darkness, wandering aimlessly, and so Handel's tone-painting is very different. Two features of the aria's music stand out: the aimlessly wandering melodic line and the sparse texture. The wandering melody, of course, depicts the people walking in darkness. The sparse texture is equally important to the "picture." The bass soloist and the strings are in unison and octaves most of the time; they have no independent parts; they create no harmony. The music sounds empty, like the dark, barren wilderness in which the people are wandering. The light in this musical picture breaks through in the modulation to major keys on "have seen a great light"; in the only long-held high note and in the only melisma, both emphasizing "light"; and in the full harmony of the short instrumental interludes that follow the word "light."

The light, of course, is the virgin's child, Emmanuel. As the Gospel of John puts it: "In him was life; and the life was the light of men. And the light shineth in darkness, and the darkness comprehended it not" (1:4-5). So this scene reaches its climax in the chorus "For unto us a child is born." Handel arranged it, like "And he shall purify," from one of his secular duet cantatas. As he did with the earlier arrangement, he retained the airy texture of the original by limiting the choir to one or two parts at a time and adding only an extremely sparse orchestral accompaniment. He saved the full choral/orchestral texture for the thrilling climax on the names that further identify the child: "Wonderful, Counsellor, the Mighty God, the Everlasting Father, the Prince of Peace."

Scene 4

13. *Orchestra:* Pifa

14. Secco *recitative:* There were shepherds abiding in the field, keeping watch over their flock by night.

    Accompanied recitative: And lo, an angel of the Lord came upon them, and the glory of the Lord shone round about them, and they were sore afraid.

15. Secco *recitative:* And the angel said unto them: Fear not, for behold, I bring you good tidings of great joy, which shall be to all people: for unto you is born this day in the city of David a Saviour, which is Christ the Lord (Luke 2:8-11).

16. *Accompanied recitative:* And suddenly there was with the angel a multitude of the heavenly host, praising God, and saying:

17. Turba *chorus:* Glory to God in the highest, and peace on earth, goodwill towards men (Luke 2:13-14).

Scene 4 is unique in *Messiah*. Until now everything has been prophecy; here we get history. Angels speak and sing to shepherds at a specific time and place. They tell of a baby born "this day in the city of David."

The scene begins with an instrumental piece that Handel called "Pifa." It is his version of the Italian words "piva" (bagpipe) and "piffero" (shawm, reed pipe). From his time in Italy he may have known of the Italian custom in which shepherds from southern Italy came to Rome during Advent, playing shawms and bagpipes. Today the piece is often called the "Pastoral Symphony." Either title indicates its function: to depict a pastoral scene.

The "Pifa" offers a good example of Handel using a stylistic convention to convey a specific meaning. Just as the rhythmic characteristics of the French overture conveyed royal pomp and splendor, so Handel's "Pifa" has musical characteristics that conveyed pastoral associations. To suggest a pastoral scene or evoke a pastoral mood, Baroque composers wrote long-held notes imitative of bagpipe drones. Above the drones they wrote simple melodies that flow along quietly and gently, usually in triple rhythms. The clear, simple harmony contains very little dissonance. In short, the music is devoid of artistic sophistication, which would be inappropriate for depicting simple shepherds. In the "Pifa" Handel followed these pastoral conventions faithfully. (See Example 3 on p. 102.)

After the "Pifa" sets the scene, a soprano narrates the story, singing alternately between *secco* recitative and accompanied recitative. The narrative begins with something that is entirely commonplace —

EXAMPLE 3

"There were shepherds abiding in the field" — sung in a most simple, matter-of-fact *secco* recitative style. But then something extraordinary happens — "And lo the angel of the Lord came upon them" — which Handel highlighted by switching to accompanied recitative. Then the angel speaks, so *secco* recitative returns to present the angel's message with utmost clarity. After the angel finishes speaking, another extraordinary thing happens — the angel is joined by a "multitude of the heavenly host." Again Handel highlighted the extraordinary event with a change to accompanied recitative. And when the angels sing "Glory to God in the highest," of course he wrote a chorus. In the *historia* tradition, this would be called a *turba* ("crowd") chorus, that is, a chorus that sets the words said by a group of characters in the story, in this case the "crowd" of angels.

"Glory to God" provided Handel with several opportunities for madrigalisms. The obvious ones include "glory" (bustling strings and, for the first time, trumpets) contrasting with "peace" (quiet unisons) and "God in the highest" (high range) contrasting with "earth" (low range and an octave leap down). Also note the gently stroked repeated notes following "peace on earth," recalling the repeated notes that permeate the accompaniment of "Comfort ye."

With no literal way to depict "goodwill" in music, it might seem at first that Handel simply resorted to writing a lively stretto fugue. However, since the entrances of the voices are so close together, the ascending leap on "goodwill" soon begins to dominate the texture. It doesn't take a whole lot of imagination to hear this as convivial greetings — "goodwill" sounding like hearty shouts of "good cheer" accompanied by the raising of glasses. This image becomes especially apparent when Handel completely isolates the word "goodwill" and tosses it around from voice to voice. (See Example 4 below.)

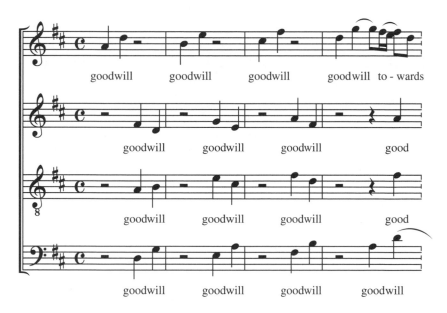

EXAMPLE 4

The story of Scene 4 is now complete, but according to Baroque operatic conventions it still needs a piece portraying the main affect generated by the story. Since joy is the affect most immediately associated with the birth of Christ, "Rejoice greatly, O daughter of Zion" provides a suitable text for that function. And the music Handel wrote for that text certainly expresses joy most exuberantly. But in the word-book for the 1743 *Messiah* performance in London, Jennens placed "Rejoice" at the beginning of Scene 5, not at the climax of Scene 4.

As we shall see, Jennens's placement of "Rejoice" in Scene 5 makes good sense, but I think we miss something if we don't hear "Rejoice" in connection with what immediately went before it as well as its connection with what follows it. Conventional expectations, the immediate meaning of the words, and the character of the music all mark it as a joyful response to the story of Christ's birth. Although an aria might sound anti-climactic following a glorious chorus, that is not the case here. "Rejoice" more than makes up for its lack of bulk with sheer virtuosity, which is largely due to the long melismas on the word "rejoice." The melismas, however, provide more than merely an impressive, virtuosic show. Melismatic singing as a conventional way to express joy has very ancient lineage. It goes back centuries before Handel's time, back at least as far as the early centuries of the church. St. Augustine called it singing "in jubilation."

> It is to grasp the fact that what is sung in the heart cannot be articulated in words. Think of people who sing at harvest time, or in the vineyard. . . . They begin by caroling their joy in words, but after a while they seem to be so full of gladness that they find words no longer adequate to express it, so they abandon distinct syllables and words, and resort to a single cry of jubilant happiness.

In such singing, he said, "the heart may tell its joy without words, and the unbounded rush of gladness [is] not cramped by syllables."[6] In "Rejoice" the expression of joy at the birth of Christ is certainly not "cramped by syllables." (See Example 5 on p. 105.)

Scene 5

18. *Aria:* Rejoice greatly, O daughter of Zion, shout, O daughter of Jerusalem, behold, thy King cometh unto thee. He is the righteous Saviour, and He shall speak peace unto the heathen (Zech. 9:9-10).

19. Secco *recitative:* Then shall the eyes of the blind be opened, and the ears of the deaf unstopped; then shall the lame man leap as an hart, and the tongue of the dumb shall sing (Isa. 35:5-6).

re-joice,_____ re-joice,_____

EXAMPLE 5

20. *Aria:* He shall feed His flock like a shepherd, and He shall gather the lambs with His arm, and carry them in His bosom, and gently lead those that are with young (Isa. 40:11). Come unto Him, all ye that labour, come unto Him all ye that are heavy laden, and He will give you rest. Take His yoke upon you, and learn of Him, for He is meek and lowly of heart, and ye shall find rest unto your souls.

21. *Chorus:* His yoke is easy, and His burthen is light (Matt. 11:28-30).

The "Rejoice" aria consists of three sections, the third being a varied repetition of the first. The key word in the first and third sections is "rejoice"; in the middle section it is "peace." In the middle section we most readily see the connection of the aria to Scene 5. This scene tells of some of the wonderful things that will happen as a result of the Messiah's birth, beginning with the peace promised in the middle section of the aria. But that promise is already hinted at in the first section of the text when it explicitly identifies the Messiah as King: "behold, thy King cometh unto thee." The overture suggested the coming of a king, but until now he has not been explicitly identified as such. However, the context of the words that make this identification, as biblically savvy listeners will recognize, reveals something unusual about this King. The prophet Zechariah, in words not included by Jennens, described this King as "lowly, and riding upon an ass, and upon a colt the foal of an ass" (Zech. 9:9b), words quoted by Matthew, Mark, and John in their telling of the story of Jesus' entry into Jerusalem. It is this lowly King who will "speak peace unto the heathen." He will bring the peace promised in "Comfort ye."

The following recitative tells some specific aspects of the peace brought by this lowly King. They are told in *secco* recitative as directly and matter-of-factly as the birth of the Messiah was told in "Behold, a virgin shall conceive." The blind will see, the deaf will hear, the lame will leap, and the dumb will sing. These miracles refer to the Messiah's work on earth. John the Baptist, while in prison, sent his disciples to ask Jesus, "Art thou he who should come?" Jesus answered, "Go and show John again those things which ye do hear and see: the blind receive their sight, and the lame walk, the lepers are cleansed, and the deaf hear, the dead are raised up, and the poor have the gospel preached to them" (Matt. 11:3-5).

The aria "He shall feed His flock" concludes the list of results by returning to the first one, peace. But here the Messiah is not depicted as a King. The one whose birth was first announced to shepherds is now depicted as the Shepherd, an image that calls to mind the peace and security of Psalm 23 and Jesus' identification of himself as the Good Shepherd who cares for his sheep (John 10:11, 14). In this aria we hear the comforting words that the Shepherd will "feed His flock, . . . gather the lambs with His arm, . . . carry them in His bosom, . . . and gently lead those that are with young."

The aria ends with an invitation. After the alto sings "He shall feed his flock," the soprano continues in a higher range, singing words Jesus said of himself (but with the pronouns changed to third person): "Come unto Him, all ye that labour, and He will give you rest." Appropriately, Handel set the comforting words and gracious invitation of this aria in the same pastoral style he used for the "Pifa." (See Example 6 on p. 107.)

The final chorus of Part I is "His yoke is easy and his burthen is light." The words continue Jesus' invitation (again with the pronouns changed to third person). The music is built on a lightly bouncing bass above which the choir sings lots of rapid runs. If they can dash these off without apparent labor, the music effectively conveys ease and

He shall feed his flock like a shep - herd,

EXAMPLE 6

lightness. Throughout the movement, another that Handel developed from a duet cantata, the texture is appropriately light and airy. But at the end, the light, rapid runs and the bouncing bass halt, the rhythm broadens, the texture thickens, a feeling of heaviness replaces the lightness that had pervaded the movement, and just before the final chord we hear a slight sting of dissonance. Why this sudden change at the end of the chorus? It calls to my mind Dietrich Bonhoeffer's *The Cost of Discipleship*. Its introduction ends, like Part I of *Messiah*, with Jesus' words: "My yoke is easy, and my burden is light." But Bonhoeffer immediately goes on in the first chapter to speak of "costly grace." Grace is costly "because it cost God the life of his Son: 'ye were bought at a price.'"[7] Part II will tell how much the grace promised in Part I cost. The gravity of the final cadence of "His yoke is easy" points ahead to Part II.

Chapter 8

Part the Second

Lamb of God, King of Kings

Scene 1

22. *Chorus:* Behold the Lamb of God
23. *Aria:* He was despised
24. *Chorus:* Surely He hath borne our griefs
25. *Chorus:* And with His stripes we are healed
26. *Chorus:* All we like sheep have gone astray
27. *Accompanied recitative:* All they that see Him, laugh Him to scorn
28. Turba *chorus:* He trusted in God that He would deliver Him
29. *Accompanied recitative:* Thy rebuke hath broken His heart
30. *Arioso:* Behold, and see if there be any sorrow like unto His sorrow

Scene 2

31. *Accompanied recitative:* He was cut off out of the land of the living
32. *Aria:* But Thou didst not leave His soul in hell

Scene 3

33. *Chorus:* Lift up your heads, O ye gates

Scene 4

34. Secco *recitative:* Unto which of the angels said He at any time:
    Thou art My Son
35. *Chorus:* Let all the angels of God worship Him

Scene 5

36. *Aria:* Thou art gone up on high
37. *Chorus:* The Lord gave the word
38. *Aria:* How beautiful are the feet of them that preach the gospel
    of peace
39. *Chorus:* Their sound has gone out into all lands

Scene 6

40. *Aria:* Why do the nations so furiously rage together
41. *Chorus:* Let us break their bonds asunder

Scene 7

42. Secco *recitative:* He that dwelleth in heaven shall laugh them
    to scorn
43. *Aria:* Thou shalt break them

Scene 8

44. *Chorus:* Hallelujah!

Unlike Part I, in which the scenes are very regular in their organization, Part II never uses the normal scene pattern — recitative, aria, chorus. Probably the first thing one notices is the disparity in size of the scenes. Scene 1 has nine numbers whereas all but one of the rest have only one or two numbers. Not only does scene size vary greatly, but structure does also. Except for the two isolated choruses (Scenes 3 and 8), only Scenes 2 and 7 have the same structure. Further, we might raise questions about Jennens's divisions, or, in the case of the big first scene, about the lack of divisions. All of this might suggest rather haphazard organization, but I hope that what follows will show that not to be the case.

Scene 1, prologue

22. *Chorus:* Behold the Lamb of God, that taketh away the sin of the world (John 1:29).

The beginning of Part II has two clear connections with the beginning of Part I. First, Part I began with a French overture, and Part II begins with a chorus permeated by the same kind of stately dotted rhythms that characterize French overtures. Second, the opening words of both parts make reference to John the Baptist. Part I prophesied John in the opening recitative as "The voice . . . that crieth in the wilderness." Part II begins with John's words heralding Jesus at the Jordan River: "Behold the Lamb of God."

The music of this chorus relates ironically to John's words. The French overture style suggests royal pomp and splendor; the words speak of a Lamb, the humble animal associated with the sacrificial lamb of the Passover. That irony is heightened if the trills marked in the violin parts are consistently applied to the analogous places in the voice parts, where they always occur on the word "Lamb." A trill on the "a" of "lamb" can sound remarkably like the bleating of a lamb. The words of this chorus also bear an ironic relationship with "He shall feed His flock," the final aria of Part I. The Shepherd of that aria is now identified as a Lamb.

The orchestra begins with the upward leap to which the choir will sing "Behold." A descending scale follows, which, along with the minor key and the halting dotted rhythms in a slow tempo, contributes a feeling of weightiness, quite the opposite of the feeling that had been given by the lightly dashed off runs in the closing chorus of Part I. His yoke *is* easy and his burden *is* light for those who come to him, but the burden of the sin he bears for them is heavy. He not only bears it; he bears it away. So at the words "that taketh away the sin of the world," the descending music turns around and ascends back up the scale. But the ascent isn't easy; it is slow and halting. Nevertheless by the end of the first half of the piece the sopranos have reached their highest pitch of the movement, and the music has modulated to a major key. But lest that makes us forget the weight of our sins, the second half of the chorus reemphasizes it. The sopranos sing "that taketh away the sin of the world" all on the same note while the lower parts trudge along in halting dotted rhythms, singing melodies that strive to ascend but never get very far. His burden on us is light; our burden on him is heavy indeed. The rest of Scene 1 will tell how heavy.

Scene 1, section 1

23. *Aria:* He was despised and rejected of men, a man of sorrows, and acquainted with grief (Isa. 53:3). He gave His back to the smiters, and His cheeks to them that plucked off the hair, He hid not His face from shame and spitting (Isa. 50:6).

24. *Chorus:* Surely He hath borne our griefs and carried our sorrows; He was wounded for our transgressions, He was bruised for our iniquities; the chastisement of our peace was upon Him.

25. *Chorus:* And with His stripes we are healed.

26. *Chorus:* All we like sheep have gone astray, we have turned ev'ry one to his own way. And the Lord hath laid on Him the iniquity of us all (Isa. 53:4-6).

As we have noted, Scene 1 is by far the largest scene in the oratorio. Its first section alone is bigger than any other entire scene — bigger and weightier. Bigger largely because of the length of the aria — it is by far the longest in *Messiah*. Weightier because the long aria is followed by three choruses in a row — all other choruses in *Messiah* stand alone. And if we look at what immediately precedes and what immediately follows this section, we find that of the first seven numbers in Part II, five of them are choruses.

Obviously, this forms the crux of the story, and Handel's settings of these texts emphasize their crucial importance. In the aria we hear what Jesus suffered, and we hear it over and over: "He was despised and rejected of men, a man of sorrows, and acquainted with grief." The key is E♭ major, but the music is anything but happy. The tempo plods, the melodic motives sigh and descend, achingly pungent dissonant chords sound on "griefs," and the orchestra can't seem to let go of the three-note sighing motive that says "de-SPIS-ed," "re-JECT-ed."

After nearly five minutes of this (already longer than all but two of the arias in *Messiah*), we get to the next part of the text: "He gave His back to the smiters, and His cheeks to them that plucked off the hair, He hid not his face from shame and spitting." The music changes completely. It is in C minor and the orchestra plays unrelenting, rapid dotted rhythms, a Baroque convention representing scourging. The music is vicious; you can almost feel the smiters' blows. After this short but extremely intense part of the aria ends, the first part, "He was despised," repeats in its entirety — five more grief-stricken minutes.

For more than ten minutes the aria has focused on *what* the Lamb of God suffered: "He was despised. . . . He was rejected. . . . He gave His back to the smiters. . . ." In the following three numbers the focus shifts to the guilty sheep *for whom* the Lamb of God suffered. Appropriately, these texts, with all their plural first-person pronouns ("Surely He hath borne <u>our</u> griefs and carried <u>our</u> sorrows," and so on) are sung by the choir.

In "Surely he hath borne our griefs," the first of this triptych of choruses, the orchestra returns to the scourging rhythm of "He gave His back to the smiters," but it drops out at the text "He was wounded for our transgressions, He was bruised for our iniquities." There the orchestra joins the voices for a sustained passage filled with dissonance and a steady rhythm that emphasizes "bruised" and "our iniquities." Then the orchestra brings back the scourging rhythm as the choir sings the final phrase: "the chastisement of our peace was upon Him."

The next chorus begins without break. It is a fugue in a severe, old-fashioned style called *stile antico* ("old style") or *stylus ecclesiasticus* ("church style"). A fugue presents its musical theme repeatedly, first in one voice, then in another, then in another, and so on throughout the piece. Therefore, we hear the text again and again as the voices take turns entering with the theme. There is also a counter theme. It carries the same words, and like the main theme it appears in one voice after another throughout the piece. Listeners cannot miss the crucial message of these words: "And with His stripes we are healed." The most striking feature of the theme is the dissonant downward leap from the highest note (on "His") to the lowest and longest note (on "stripes"). Every time the theme is stated, that dissonant leap stands out and emphasizes what it took to heal us — "His stripes." (See Example 7 below.)

And   with His   stripes   we   are   heal - ed.

EXAMPLE 7

The third chorus in the triptych brings about a startling change. In contrast to the F minor of the previous two choruses, it is in F major, with a fast tempo, simple harmonies devoid of dissonance, and an airy and uncomplicated texture. It is, in fact, another one of the choruses Handel arranged from a secular duet cantata, and he did nothing to change the frivolous character of that music. It is hard to imagine music that stands in greater contrast to the seriousness and gravity of the preceding choruses. And yet the text offers a confession of sin: "All we like sheep have gone astray." This has puzzled, indeed troubled, many listeners. What was Handel thinking? How could he compose something so trivial, something so affectively inappropriate for a confession of sin?

In order to understand "All we like sheep," we need to make a conceptual shift. In the preceding choruses (and, for that matter, generally throughout *Messiah*), Handel, through the music, conveyed the proper "tone" for speaking (singing) the words; or, to put it another way, the music conveyed the proper attitude of the speaker (singer). In "All we like sheep," however, Handel does not aim to convey an appropriate tone of confession or the proper attitude of the confessor; rather, he tries to convey the nature of the thing being confessed. As a confession of sin, "All we like sheep" is a disaster. There's not the slightest hint of seriousness, not an ounce of contrition, in its tone. But as a depiction of the nature of sin (or at least one aspect of it) it is most apt.

Sinners can be easily romanticized as bold, even heroic, rebels.

But in reality they are like silly sheep. In this text we confess that we are all sheep, and as Bullard reminds us,

> This is not a romantic image; it is drawn from the realism of live-stock culture. It is not a picture of cuddly innocence. We are small. We are helpless against predators. We fall into rushing streams and are washed away. We wander away from the safety of the flock and the shepherd. We do silly things.[1]

Handel's music perfectly depicts the silliness of wandering away from the Shepherd. The melodic lines wander this way and that, and sometimes they stupidly turn around and around, going nowhere. In the end all the voices come together, and unaware of the irony between what they are saying and how they are saying it (that is, all together), they stubbornly insist that they "have turned every one to his own way." But even so, "the Lord hath laid on Him the iniquity of us all." (See Example 8 on p. 115.)

The music for that last line of text takes an even more dramatic turn than the change from "And with His stripes" to "All we like sheep." Indeed, it is one of the more dramatic changes in the history of music. F minor returns like a wall of doom. The music moves in tortu-ously slow, descending half-notes as the voices enter, piling one atop the other in inexorable layers of crushing weight, singing "and the Lord has laid on Him." When they get to "Him," they hold their note (the basses hold it for fourteen slow beats!). Then again they sing "hath laid on Him, hath laid on Him" — pausing together on "Him." Finally they complete the sentence, slowly and all together, and with an excru-ciating dissonance at the end of "us" —

"the in-i-qui-TY____OF_____US_____ALL_____."

Scene 1, section 2

27. *Accompanied recitative:* All they that see Him laugh Him to scorn; they shoot out their lips, and shake their heads, saying:

EXAMPLE 8

28. Turba *chorus:* He trusted in God that He would deliver Him; let Him deliver Him, if He delight in Him! (Ps. 22:7-8).

29. *Accompanied recitative:* Thy rebuke hath broken His heart; He is full of heaviness. He looked for some to have pity on Him, but there was no man, neither found He any to comfort Him (Ps. 69:20).

30. *Arioso:* Behold, and see if there be any sorrow like unto His sorrow! (Lam. 1:12).

In the prophetic texts that make up the first section of Scene 1 we followed Christ down the road of suffering he took, bearing the punishment for our sins. In the second section we follow him further down that road. The texts of section 1 parallel incidents recounted in the New Testament that occurred during Jesus' trials. Matthew says, "they did spit in his face, and buffeted him" (26:67) and "when he [Pilate] had scourged Jesus, he delivered him to be crucified" (27:26). Now in section 2, the prophetic texts parallel a New Testament incident that occurred during Jesus' time on the cross. Again Matthew:

> And they that passed by reviled him, wagging their heads, and saying, Thou that destroyest the temple, and buildest it in three days, save thyself. If thou be the Son of God, come down from the cross. Likewise also the chief priests mocking him, with the scribes and elders, said, He saved others; himself he cannot save. If he be the King of Israel, let him now come down from the cross, and we will believe him. He trusted in God; let him deliver him now, if he will have him: for he said, I am the Son of God (27:39-43).

Handel has structured this section like a scene in a Passion. The recitatives function like those of the Evangelist in a Passion, the chorus becomes a *turba* chorus, and the arioso gives a believer's response to what has just happened.

In "All they that see Him" the scourging rhythm of "He gave His back to the smiters" and "Surely He hath borne our griefs" returns. The venomous words of the mockers in this section are just as vicious as the blows of the smiters in section 1. The mocking tone of the recitative continues into the chorus. Like "And with His stripes," it is a fugue, but in every other way the two choruses stand in stark contrast to each other; "He trusted in God" is certainly not a *stylus ecclesiasticus* fugue! We particularly notice the mockery when the phrases "let Him deliver Him" and "if He delight in Him" are tossed about from voice to voice and in the sarcastic melismas on "delight."

Immediately after this outburst, the prophetic words of Psalm 69 turn our attention to the effect of all this on Jesus: "Thy rebuke hath broken His heart." Henry Hammond paraphrased the verse as follows:

> And this is it that so extremely pricks and wounds Him, that makes His sorrow so comfortless and unsupportable, that when He prayed for the expected relief from thee, He has yet been disappointed, and so scoft at by His enemies for the vanity of His hopes, which being reposed on thee, have not as yet been answered by thee.[2]

This text calls to mind Jesus' words on the cross: "My God, my God, why hast thou forsaken me?" (Matt. 27:46). Those who know Psalm 69 well will realize that its next words (v. 21, not included in the libretto) call to mind even more clearly other words that Jesus uttered on the cross: "They gave me also gall for my meat, and in my thirst they gave me vinegar to drink." The one who said "I thirst" is

> the one who turned water into wine. . . . This is the one who told the woman at the well in Samaria, "Those who drink of the water that I will give them will never be thirsty. The water that I will give will become in them a spring of water gushing up to eternal life" (John 4:14). The . . . irony is never more evident than when the one who offers humanity the water of life dies in thirst, with the sour taste of vinegar on his tongue.
>
> Such was the pity shown him. Such was his dying comfort.[3]

Donald Burrows points out that Handel used the most conventional type of accompanied recitative, which he describes as "a sustained wash of string chords," only three times in *Messiah*. Their rarity makes them all the more effective. Two of them "bear the high-point of the Passion tragedy."[4] The first one is "Thy rebuke hath broken His heart." In it the "wash of string chords" is particularly anguishing harmonically. It starts in A♭ major (four flats), but by the time it reaches the first cadence (just seven measures in) it has modulated all the way to E major (four sharps). The sharp keys perhaps point symbolically to the crucifixion, since in German, Handel's native language, the musical sharp was called "Kruez" ("cross"). For the rest of the movement it stays in sharp keys, but never securely in one place for long, and not without an occasional surprising chord in flats.

The effect of the unsettled harmonies is, in a word, heartbreaking. But the following arioso reaches beyond tears. Michael Linton describes it as "a model of economy and pathos. In its fifteen measures Handel seems to set the anguish of the whole world."[5] It bids us to look on the unparalleled sorrow of the Messiah hanging on the cross: "Behold, and see if there be any sorrow like unto His sorrow." The key word is "behold." The tenor sings it four times, always to an upward leap — "be-HOLD." The last time he sings it, the word leaps up to the soloist's highest note in the arioso. In addition to the emphatic "beholds" explicitly sung by the voice, the orchestra "says" it over and over. While the voice sings the other words, the strings repeatedly play the upward leap that says "behold."

Scene 2

31. *Accompanied recitative:* He was cut off out of the land of the living, for the transgression of Thy people was He stricken (Isa. 53:8).

32. *Aria:* But Thou didst not leave His soul in Hell; nor didst Thou suffer Thy Holy One to see corruption (Ps. 16:10).

The Messiah dies. The end (in both senses) of his suffering is death, "the last enemy" (1 Cor. 15:26). In *Messiah* little ado is made over it. Five short measures of recitative simply announce the fact — "He was cut off out of the land of the living" — and state why — "for the transgression of Thy people was he stricken." After so much time has been spent on Jesus' suffering, why so little on the death itself? In one way the question answers itself. Death is the end, what more is there to say?

Proportionally, *Messiah* is similar to the Gospel accounts of Jesus' suffering and death. Matthew's account of Jesus' death, for example, is at least as laconic as *Messiah*'s. One hundred twenty-four verses lead up to Matthew's brief death announcement: "Jesus, when he had cried again with a loud voice, yielded up his spirit" (27:50). To be sure, Matthew goes on to relate a few things that happened in the aftermath of Jesus' death, up to and including the resurrection and his final words to the disciples just before his ascension. But compared to the number of verses devoted to Jesus' final week of suffering, the post-death events receive very little attention — just thirty-six verses.

Messiah has a longer story to tell. It has no time for details like the earthquake, the burial, and the guard at the tomb. Of course it will tell of Jesus' resurrection and ascension, for incredibly, in Jesus' case death was not the end. And because it was not the end for him, it need not be the end for us.

Jesus' resurrection is told by way of Psalm 16:10. Peter used this verse in his sermon at Pentecost.

> [Jesus Christ] Whom God hath raised up, having loosed the pains of death: because it was not possible that he should be holden of it. For David speaketh concerning him, I foresaw the Lord always before my face, for he is on my right hand, that I should not be moved: Therefore did my heart rejoice, and my tongue was glad; moreover also my flesh shall rest in hope: Because thou wilt not leave my soul in hell neither wilt thou suffer thine Holy One to see corruption. (Acts 2:240-27)

Paul, preaching in Antioch, also referred to this psalm: "Wherefore he saith also in another psalm, Thou shalt not suffer thine Holy One to see corruption" (Acts 13:35).

Until now the music of Part II has been overwhelmingly in minor keys. The transition to major takes place already in the recitative "He was cut off." Despite this foretaste, the full-blown A major of the aria "But thou didst not leave" is like full sunlight after a long night. Jens Peter Larsen says it well:

> From the beginning of the aria we are in a new world, above all earthly torment and death, freed from darkness and the oppression of Hell. . . .

The bright, airy, loosened impression of this aria is chiefly derived — apart from the effects of the key and the changes of key —
from the quite simple harmonies, the light, flowing melodies and,
above all from the effect of the "running" bass. . . .[6]

Following the aria, the choir sings "Lift up your heads, O ye
gates." Given the normal recitative-aria-chorus pattern that Handel
had established in Part I, and the celebratory character of this chorus,
many hear it as the culmination of the resurrection scene. The chorus,
says Bullard, "hymns the resurrection of Messiah, the Anointed
One."[7]

A felt need to celebrate the resurrection with more than a modest
aria, be it ever so joyous and beautiful, no doubt prompts the frequent
association of "Lift up your heads" with the celebration of Christ's resurrection. As Larsen describes it, the chorus is a perfect complement to
the aria.

Immediately after the aria comes the chorus "Lift up your heads,"
one of the grand choruses of the work. Although the aria and chorus are very closely connected in content they are very different in
style. They both rejoice at the victory over Hell, but the joys differ
in character and they are very differently expressed. In the aria it is
the spontaneous joy experienced when a long-sustained pressure
abates at last. This is the joy of a father at the return of the prodigal
son, or the joy of a nation on first hearing the news of liberation after an occupation: for the moment all thought of what is to come is
suspended, unrestrained happiness fills life and existence. But the
chorus is a conscious manifestation of gratitude and jubilation, an
acclamation to the conqueror at his entry into the city. It is far
more a question of an organized act of homage.[8]

But Jennens placed "Lift up your heads" in a separate scene by itself, separated from the recitative and aria, no doubt because he associated it with Jesus' ascension rather than his resurrection.

Scene 3

33. *Chorus:* Lift up your heads, O ye gates, and be ye lift up, ye ever-lasting doors, and the King of Glory shall come in. Who is this King of Glory? The Lord strong and mighty, the Lord mighty in battle. Lift up your heads, O ye gates, and be ye lift up, ye ever lasting doors, and the King of Glory shall come in. Who is the King of Glory? The Lord of Hosts, He is the King of Glory (Ps. 24:7-10).

The Book of Common Prayer designated Psalm 24 for Evensong on Ascension Day, and Hammond explicitly says that verses 7-10 "belong to the ascension of Christ our Saviour into the highest heavens; and so the ancient Fathers frequently apply it."[9] Originally, the "gates" proba-bly referred to the gates of Jerusalem, and the antiphonal questions and answers suggest some kind of liturgical procession — perhaps as part of the celebration of David bringing the Ark into Jerusalem (2 Sam. 6). A New Testament parallel is Revelation 21:12-13, which describes the gates of the heavenly Jerusalem.

These verses then depict a scene of a victorious king returning from battle. The Messiah, the Good Shepherd, the Lamb of God, is the King of Glory returning from his victory over Satan, sin, and death.

The chorus that Handel wrote for this celebration is unique among *Messiah* choruses; it is the work's only antiphonal chorus. Han-del did not actually score it for two choirs. He scored it for a single five-part choir (SSATB), but that gave him enough voice parts to cre-ate antiphonal effects. The middle voices (altos) simply do double duty. They sing the lowest part of the high three-part choir (SSA) and the highest part of the low three-part choir (ATB).

Antiphony, of course, was dictated by the structure of the text.

SSA: Lift up your heads, O ye gates, and be ye lift up, ye everlasting doors, and the King of Glory shall come in!
TB: Who is this King of Glory?
SSA: The Lord strong and mighty, the Lord mighty in battle.

ATB: Lift up your heads, O ye gates, and be ye lift up, ye everlasting doors, and the King of Glory shall come in!

SSA: Who is this King of Glory?

ATB: The Lord of Hosts, He is the King of Glory!

Dotted rhythms characterize most of the music of this antiphonal dialogue. As in the overture and "Behold the Lamb of God," these rhythms suggest a royal entrance. But now, unlike the previous entrances, the entrance is clearly a victorious one. The minor keys and slower pace (ponderous, in the case of "Behold the Lamb of God") are gone. Gone too, it should be added, is the vicious snap of the scourging dotted rhythms. This is a victory march in F major with a lively, but stately, ceremonial step.

Handel employed a different rhythm, however, for the words "and the King of Glory shall come in." Both rhythmically and melodically that line is reminiscent of (indeed almost identical to) "and all flesh shall see it together" from the first chorus of the oratorio, "And the Glory of the Lord." Recall that Handel also wrote nearly the same music for "get thee up into the high mountain" and "say unto the cities of Judah" from "O thou that tellest good tidings to Zion." Is it far-fetched to hear, at this victorious entrance of the King of Glory, Handel's music subtly telling us that all flesh now *has* seen it [that is, the glory of the Lord] together? And that from the "high mountain," in antiphonal choirs, they *are* singing "unto the cities of Judah: Behold, your God"?

After the antiphonal dialogue, the five-part choir merges into a standard four-part choir in which the voices affirm together, "the Lord of Hosts, He is the King of Glory." But the antiphony remains, now between the choir and the orchestra.

Choir: He is the King of Glory   He is the King of Glory.
Orchestra: [He is the King of Glory]   [He is the King of Glory]

Then the text continues, but it is sung to a new musical theme characterized by a strong upward leap to "Hosts," and long melismas on "Glory." The texture becomes somewhat fugal but it always returns to antiphony between the choir and the orchestra.

This grand and thrilling chorus ends with three long, strong chords — "of GLO-RY" — the final two being the traditional chords for "Amen."

Scene 4

34. Secco *recitative:* Unto which of the angels said He at any time: Thou art My Son, this day have I begotten thee?

35. *Chorus:* Let all the angels of God worship Him (Heb. 1:5-6).

A case could be made that Scenes 2, 3, and 4 belong together as one long scene comparable to Scene 1. Just as Scene 1 traced Christ's humiliation from John the Baptist's introduction of him as the sacrificial Lamb of God, through his suffering and trials, to his death on the cross, so Scenes 2 through 4 trace his exaltation from his resurrection, through his ascension, to his being acclaimed Son of God and worshipped by the angels — the subject of Scene 4.

The recitative from Hebrews 1:5 quotes from Psalm 2, which "may well have been composed for the enthronement of a king. . . . [In verse 7] God speaks to the new king: You are my son; today I have begotten you."[10] The same verse appears in Acts 13:33. There "Paul quotes it in the context of a sermon he delivers on one of his missionary journeys. There the application is made to the resurrection and exaltation of Jesus."[11]

The text of the chorus is from the next verse of Hebrews 1, which exhorts the angels to worship the Son. The speaker is still God the Father. The angels obey by singing a musically sophisticated chorus, the words serving as both God's exhortation and the angels' response. (That combination isn't uncommon in singing. Think, for example, of the children's song, "Praise him, praise him, all you little children.") Without orchestral introduction, the choir and orchestra together issue the exhortation simply and directly in a strong, declamatory style: "Let all the angels of God worship him." The violins begin the response by playing two measures alone, which turn out to be the two themes of a double fugue. The main theme is the melody the sopranos sang in the opening exhortation, now played by the second violins. At the same time the first violins play the second theme, which turns out to be the first theme played twice as fast (all of which Handel "borrowed" from a keyboard fugue by Johann Kaspar Kerll). (See Example 9 below.)

[Let all the an-gels of God]

[Let   all   the   an-gels of God]

EXAMPLE 9

Next the sopranos and altos join in with the two themes. Throughout the piece, different pairs of voices state the two themes in different keys, alternating which theme is above and which is below. Handel (with the aid of Kerll) has the angelic choir singing some highly sophisticated music in their worship of the Son of God!

Scene 5

36. *Aria:* Thou art gone up on high, Thou hast led captivity captive, and received gifts for men, yea, even for Thine enemies, that the Lord God might dwell among them (Ps. 68:18).

37. *Chorus:* The Lord gave the word, great was the company of the preachers (Ps. 68:11).

38. *Aria:* How beautiful are the feet of them that preach the gospel of peace and bring glad tidings of good things (Rom. 10:15).

39. *Chorus:* Their sound is gone out into all the lands, and their words unto the ends of the world (Rom. 10:18).

Although the transition from Scene 4 to Scene 5 marks a distinct change of location (literally from heaven to earth), the transition is made smoothly in the aria "Thou art gone up on high." The first phrase refers to Jesus' ascension into heaven, but by the third phrase the focus has shifted to "men."

Read as a prophecy of Christ, the first part of the text is readily understood: Christ ascended victoriously into heaven, leading captives in his train — indeed, leading captivity itself captive. But the next phrase may be a little confusing. The Book of Common Prayer translation, which is what Jennens chose here, says "and received gifts for men," whereas in Ephesians 4:8, which quotes Psalm 68:18, the King James translation (which, of course, Jennens also knew) reads "and gave gifts for men." Either way, it seems clear that the point Jennens wanted to make is that when the victorious Christ entered heaven he received gifts, which he gave to humankind. As Hammond put it in his commentary on the Ephesians verse, "At his [Christ's] ascension, he carried Satan, sin and death captive, and scattered many several gifts and extraordinary graces by sending the holy Ghost upon his disciples, as Elias did upon Elishah at his ascent."[12]

It seems likely, given Hammond's reference to the Holy Spirit, that Jennens also meant this verse to bring to mind the birth of the church at Pentecost (Whitsunday). In addition, Jennens knew the Scripture readings of the Book of Common Prayer very well and certainly would have known that Psalm 68 was assigned to Matins on Whitsunday. He must have had in mind both the association of Psalm 68 with Whitsunday and the context of the quotation from the psalm in Ephesians when he chose the next three texts in this scene, all of which have to do with the spread of the gospel throughout the world — "Preached among the Gentiles" as the motto has it. Ephesians 4 goes on to say,

Now that he ascended, what is it but that he also descended first into the lower parts of the earth? He that descended is the same also that ascended up farre above all heavens, that he might fill all things. And he gave some Apostles, and some Prophets, and some Evangelists, and some Pastors and Teachers (vss. 9-11).

Hammond's paraphrase of verses 10 and 11 reads:

> His ascending again, though it were for a time the leaving of us, yet it was designed to the sending down the holy Ghost upon the Apostles, by that means to supply all our wants, to doe what was necessary to be done to the planting and governing of his Church. And to that end he hath constituted some to be founders and governours of all Churches . . . others to teach and confirm them when they are founded . . . others, followers of the Apostles, sent to preach the Gospel, where the Apostles could not go . . . others to reside as Bishops, and govern particular Churches, and instruct them also.[13]

Musically, this scene gets off to a weak start. Although the music of the aria is attractive, it seems to have little connection to the text. Critics have called it "abstract" (Larsen) and "neutral" (Burrows). Larsen says that Handel "is less involved" and lays the blame on "textual obscurity."[14] It may be true that the text is to blame, but I doubt that its meaning or purpose was obscure to Handel. It seems more likely that he simply found nothing in the text to fire his musical imagination. Not all texts lend themselves to vivid musical portrayal. As Burrows puts it:

> As regards expressive content, a rough distinction may be made between movements which are "text-led" (putting over the emotional message of the text as forcefully as possible) and those which are "music-led" (setting the text appropriately, but evolving the movement primarily through extension, development and contrast in musical ideas). . . . Since [*Messiah*] required a number of abstract texts: by his treatment of these, Handel introduced a variety and equilibrium into the work's musical and dramatic elements. He was not simply making the best of a bad job.[15]

The text might have been better set as a recitative, which could have better served its function as a transition. At least a recitative would be much shorter and therefore would be less likely to be cut, as is so often done in modern performances. Cutting this text, as Larsen says, "is hardly defensible. It is a necessary link in the general plan of the work, and by his repeated recastings of the aria Handel has shown that he always retained it in spite of the difficulties it caused him."[16]

Handel had no such difficulties with the next three texts of this scene. They all celebrate the same thing, the spread of the gospel, but they all celebrate a different aspect of it. In the first chorus, everything in the music speaks of strength: the opening unison declaration by the tenors and basses ("The Lord gave the word"); the march-like declamation in solid four-part harmony with all the voice parts doubled at the octave in the orchestra; and the rising sixteenth-note melismas. As Larsen puts it: "Strong in their conviction of victory, irresistible, God's messengers set out to preach . . . that mankind has been liberated from the power of Death."[17] Next a lovely aria depicts the beauty of the message. It features the gentle, graceful rhythms of a *siciliano*, a dance with pastoral associations. And the final chorus, beginning with all the voices in succession singing a trumpet call ("Their sound is gone out"), illustrates the extent of the gospel's spread with scales running up and down. These scales always traverse an octave, a Baroque convention signifying everything, or, in this case everywhere — from north to south, from east to west.

Scene 6

40. *Aria:* Why do the nations so furiously rage together, and why do the people imagine a vain thing? The kings of the earth rise up, and the rulers take counsel together against the Lord and against his anointed.

41. *Chorus:* Let us break their bonds asunder, and cast away their yokes from us (Ps. 2:1-3).

The gospel has gone out to all the world, but all the world does not accept it. Kings and nations rise up and rebel "against the Lord and against his anointed," the Messiah. What happened to the promises heard in Part I? The Messiah was called "Prince of Peace," and his coming was heralded by angels singing of "peace on earth." Now he has come, and yet there is no peace. The Prince of Peace himself said, "Think not that I am come to send peace on earth: I came not to send peace, but a sword" (Matt. 10:34). He who conquered the forces that had captured humankind — Satan and sin and death — he who "led captivity captive," knew that not all would accept the freedom he won for them. He whose "yoke is easy" knew that some would rise up to cast off his yoke. "Non serviam" ("I will not serve") has been the cry of rebels from the beginning of time. In *Paradise Lost* Satan says, "Better to reign in Hell, then serve in Heav'n" (Book I, l. 263). God, through Jeremiah (2:20), accused Israel of refusing to serve him: "For of old time I have broken thy yoke, and burst thy bands; and thou saidst, [in the Latin Vulgate translation] 'non serviam.'" God broke the bonds with which Egypt held Israel captive; yet they turned from him. And now, even after the Messiah has come and "led captivity captive," still "the kings of the earth rise up . . . against the Lord and against his anointed, [saying:] 'Let us break their bonds asunder.'"

This is the epitome of a "rage" aria. The blistering fast repeated notes in the strings are classic *stile concitato*, the agitated, war-like style. The bass soloist enters in the most powerful part of his range and mounts up through a C major chord to the top of his range to accent "so FU — rious-ly RAGE to-ge-ther." When he gets to "rage" the second time, it takes very little imagination to hear him trembling with rage on the long melisma.

The music continues in that vein throughout the first part, and in Handel's original version, it continues in similar fashion through the next part, "The kings of the earth rise up. . . ." He set up the second part to end in such a way that listeners will expect a return of the first part. In other words, he set it up to be a typical aria in da capo form (A-B-A). But just at the moment when we expect a return to the be-ginning, the choir jumps in with "Let us break their bonds asunder." The surprise entrance of the choir is a stroke of dramatic genius. The music of the chorus vividly depicts the verbs — "break" with jagged, broken melodic lines, and "cast away" with long, descending melismas.

The anger of the aria is replaced by an almost jocular bravura as kings and nations anticipate their triumph.

Before the first performance, Handel had already revised his original version of the aria. He shortened the first part and turned the second part into a short recitative, thus eliminating the expectation of a return of the first part, and with it, the surprising, dramatic entry of the choir. We do not know his reason for the change, but some suspect that the bass soloist for the first performance in Dublin was not up to the task of performing such a long, virtuosic aria. Unfortunately, it seems that Handel, in repeated performances, never returned to his original version. Did he never have a bass soloist capable of singing it well? That seems unlikely. But it also seems unlikely that Handel preferred the shortened version. As John Tobin asks,

> who could imagine that Handel, a sensitive artist and craftsman, would . . . allow the completely satisfying and expressive tripartite structure . . . to be wrecked by such a stop-gap as this truncated, misshapen alternative in which . . . we are suddenly switched to a closing recitative of seven bars, in itself a dramatic recitative but a poor substitute for the final fifty-eight bars of one of the finest of Handel's "rage" arias?[18]

Scene 7

42. Secco *recitative:* He that dwelleth in heaven shall laugh them to scorn; the Lord shall have them in derision (Ps. 2:4).

43. *Aria:* Thou shalt break them with a rod of iron. Thou shalt dash them in pieces like a potter's vessel (Ps. 2:9).

The scene now shifts back to heaven. God views the jocular bravura of the rebels as a "vain thing"; he "shall laugh them to scorn." A short recitative leads effectively into a vengeful aria in which Handel emphasized the verbs "break" and "dash." The violins' melody is broken up by large leaps. It starts high with a fast, quavering motive, which might depict shaking with rage or derisive laughter — or both. Then follows a large downward leap to two accented eighth notes. (See Example 10 below.)

EXAMPLE 10

The instrumental bass part and the voice part are full of rests that literally break their melodic lines into little pieces. In the voice part the words "BREAK them," "DASH them," and "PIE-ces" invariably occur on downward leaps, illustrative of throwing down, dashing to the ground. (See Example 11 below.)

Thou   shalt   dash   them   in   piec - es

EXAMPLE 11

The aria is built over an ostinato bass — a short pattern of notes in the bass that repeats throughout the piece. In this case, the bass notes follow a conventional pattern that consists of a stepwise descent, either diatonically (A-G-F-E) or chromatically (A-G♯-G-F♯-F-E). (See Example 10 on p. 130.) Handel used both versions of the pattern in this aria, repeating them in various keys. This Baroque musical convention is usually associated with lamentation. Henry Purcell's "Dido's Lament" offers a well-known example; another is the "Crucifixus" from Bach's *Mass in B Minor*. But in Handel's aria the forcefully accented rhythms of the bass part obliterate any hint of lament or pity, calling to mind God's words in Jeremiah 13:14: "And I will dash them one against another, even the fathers and the sons together, saith the Lord, I will not pity, nor spare, nor have mercy, but destroy them." Those who mocked Jesus on the cross, those who had no pity on him, now become the objects of God's derision and lack of pity.

Something disturbs us about this. But that is how Jennens's chosen text portrays God, and Handel did nothing to mollify us or gloss over the image; if anything he sharpened it! This angry, vengeful God would not be disturbing if he were not real. An angry, mythological god in an opera might produce an entertaining *frisson* but no real disturbance. But Jennens and Handel believed in the reality of the God they portrayed, and they hoped to convince the Deists, atheists, and complacent Christians in their audience that this angry God is "dreadfully provoked," and that "his wrath . . . burns like fire."

Those last words come from Jonathan Edwards's most famous, or notorious, sermon, "Sinners in the Hands of an Angry God." (Coincidentally, he preached it on 8 July 1741, just two days before Jennens wrote to Holdsworth saying that he hoped to persuade Handel "to set another. . . . The Subject is Messiah.")[19] "Thou shalt break them" is in some ways a Jennens/Handel version of "Sinners in the Hands of an Angry God." Both depict an angry God "who must condemn sinners because they are in rebellion against God and hence hate what is truly good."[20] Although in Edwards's sermon, as George Marsden points out, "being in the hands of God means for the moment you are being kept from burning in hell as you deserve," and the sermon ends with "a note of hope that was ultimately the point of the sermon," we should still not be surprised that Isaac Watts called it "A most terrible sermon, which should have had a word of Gospel at the end [of] it, though I think 'tis all true." Marsden comments, "Indeed if one [takes] this ser-

mon as characteristic of his preaching, it [is] dreadfully out of balance"[21] unless it is taken in the context of Edwards's preaching as a
whole. "Thou shalt break them" is likewise out of balance unless it is
taken in the context of *Messiah* as a whole, for in it God's love far over-
shadows his anger.

"Thou shalt break them" might be criticized for identifying the
objects of God's wrath too generally (and all too conveniently) as
"them." "He . . . shall laugh them to scorn; the Lord shall have them in
derision. Thou shalt break them. . . . Thou shalt dash them in
pieces. . . ." Edwards, by contrast, very pointedly identified his listeners
as the objects of God's wrath. "[H]is wrath towards you burns like fire
. . . he looks upon you as worthy . . . to be cast into the fire. . . . You
have offended him infinitely more than ever a stubborn rebel did his
prince. . . ."[22] Listeners to *Messiah* will not necessarily deflect guilt
away from themselves onto others, but that is a natural tendency, especially while repeatedly hearing "them . . . them . . . them." Further,
Messiah as a whole won't provide much help in combating that natural
tendency. Ruth Smith says that two theological elements "are notably
absent from *Messiah:* a sense of individual worthlessness or sin, and a
concept of judgement in which the sinner is consigned to hell. . . .
Those to be 'dashed to pieces' are always 'them,' and the audience is
not, unlike the congregation of Bach's Passions, implicated in the de-
nial of Christ."[23]

Though Smith's observation is largely true, those elements are
not entirely absent. The explicit confession of guilt in "All we like
sheep have gone astray" is communal, and the "iniquities of us all" and
the "sins of the world" surely include those of the listener. And although the text makes no mention of hell as punishment for those sins,
to be broken "with a rod of iron" and dashed "in pieces like a potter's
vessel" are images of severe punishment. Admittedly neither a deep
sense of individual sin nor a concept of punishment in hell is explicit in
Messiah; nothing in it confronts us with the magnitude of our sin and
its consequences to the degree that Edwards's sermon and Bach's Passions do. But *Messiah* does not skimp in portraying the suffering and
death of the Messiah, and nothing speaks more powerfully than that to
the seriousness of sin and its dire consequences.

To the criticism that this scene does nothing to discourage the human tendency to deflect guilt from self to "others," we can add the disquieting possibility that many in Handel's audiences may have understood "them" to refer to some very specific "others." In particular, Michael Marissen points out that many Christians took "them" in Psalm 2 to be the Jews who did not believe that Jesus was the Messiah. Further, they took the breaking and dashing in verse 9 to refer to the fall of Jerusalem and the destruction of the Temple in A.D. 70.[24] For example, Matthew Henry, commenting on Psalm 2:9 wrote: "*Thou shalt break them* . . . was in part fulfill'd when the Nation of the *Jews*, those that persisted in Unbelief and Enmity to CHRIST's Gospel were destroy'd by the *Roman* power, which was represented, *Dan.* ii.40. by *Feet of Iron*, as here by *a Rod of Iron*."[25]

Henry Hammond's commentary is similar.

[Those who do] not acknowledge his divine power, now he is risen from the dead, but continue to provoke him still, they will certainly have their portion with his enemies, be destroyed with the Jews, or after the like manner, that the Jews were, when the Romans came in, and wrought a horrid desolation among them. . . .[26]

Jennens probably agreed with Henry and Hammond. But does that mean he intended "them" in "Thou shalt break them" to refer to Jews? Only, or especially, to Jews? Or to Jews among all others who deny Jesus as the Messiah? If he was intending to teach what Hammond and Henry taught, the answers are: Perhaps especially, but definitely not only, to the Jews; and yes, most certainly, to all who deny Jesus as the Messiah. Hammond and Henry, in their commentaries on Psalm 2, do not talk about the Jews as the only enemies of Christ or the only recipients of God's punishment. Hammond consistently refers to the enemies as Jews and Romans. Henry refers to them more broadly — for example, "Adversaries of Christ," "Devil's Instruments" — and these categories include "Princes and People, Court and Country"; and "Not the *Mighty* only, but the *Mob*, the *Heathen*, the *People*." The battle is between "Hell and Heaven," between "the Seed of the Serpent" and "the Seed of the Woman." And in referring to the fall of Jerusalem as God's punishment on the Jews, Henry immediately added that the prophecy of Psalm 2:9 was "further accomplished in the Destruction of the *Pagan* Powers, when the Christian Religion came to be establish'd [by Constantine]; but it will not be completely fulfill'd till all opposing Rule, Principallity and Power shall be finally put down."[27]

But Jennens's intentions aside, who are "they," those enemies of Christ who will be (or have been) broken "with a rod of iron" and dashed "in pieces like a potter's vessel"? According to *Messiah*, they are those who "take counsel against the Lord and His anointed," that is, those who did not and do not listen to the "company of the preachers" whose "sound is gone out into all lands" with "the gospel of peace" — the gospel that Jesus Christ is the Messiah.

Scene 8

44. *Chorus:* Hallelujah! For the Lord God Omnipotent reigneth! Hallelujah! The Kingdom of this world is become the Kingdom of our Lord and of His Christ, and He shall reign forever and ever. King of Kings and Lord of Lords (Rev. 19:6, 11:15, 19:16).

The "Hallelujah" in Revelation 19:6 is the third hallelujah in that chapter. Chapter 18 describes the fall of Babylon. The first two hallelujahs in chapter 19 celebrate that fall.

> And after these things I heard a great voice of much people in heaven, saying, Alleluia; Salvation, and glory, and honour, and power, unto the Lord our God: For true and righteous are his judgements; for he hath judged the great whore, which did corrupt the earth with her fornication, and hath avenged the blood of his servants at her hand.
>
> And again they said, Alleluia. And her smoke rose up for ever and ever. (vss. 1-3)

The third hallelujah introduces the marriage of the Lamb:

And I heard as it were the voice of a great multitude, and as the voice of many waters, and as the voice of mighty thunderings, saying, Alleluia: for the Lord God omnipotent reigneth. Let us be glad and rejoice, and give honour to him; for the marriage of the Lamb is come. . . . (vss. 6-7)

In *Messiah* the famous "Hallelujah Chorus" follows immediately upon the victory over the rebellious kings and nations. In that way it can be understood as rejoicing over the fall of Christ's enemies, just as the first two hallelujahs in Revelation 19 rejoiced over the fall of Babylon. But that fall of those who rebel "against the Lord and His anointed" is not only, or even mainly, what the "Hallelujah Chorus" celebrates. Like the third hallelujah of Chapter 19, it expresses joy at a great, solemn event — in Revelation 19 it is the marriage of the Lamb; in *Messiah* it is the coronation of the Lamb as King. The Lamb of God, who suffered and died to take away the sin of the world, who was raised from the dead, and who ascended to heaven, is the King of Kings and Lord of Lords who will reign for ever and ever. In the plan of *Messiah*, the "Hallelujah Chorus" is not merely the culmination of a scene; it is a scene unto itself, the culmination of the entire Part II, indeed of the whole oratorio to this point.

In 1727, Handel had written four anthems for the coronation ceremonies of King George II and Queen Caroline. Here he has time for only one, this coronation being part of a long story that must be told in one evening's entertainment. But that posed no problem for Handel. In this single three and one-half minute "coronation anthem" he packed all the jubilation and solemnity necessary for the occasion.

The piece begins with the orchestra stating one of two "hallelujah" motives (HAL-le-lu-jah) that will continually reappear throughout the movement. The choir picks up that motive, repeats it, and then introduces a second, quicker "hallelujah" motive (hal-le-LU-jah). The excitement built by repetitions of both motives is enhanced by antiphonal answers to the quick motive in the orchestra.

Choir: hal-le-LU-jah   hal-le-LU-jah
Orchestra: [hal-le-LU-jah]   [hal-le-LU-jah]

After the lively, jubilant introduction, the reason for singing hallelujah is given: "for the Lord God Omnipotent reigneth." The choir
sings this in unison to a majestic, ceremonial melody, most notable for
the big tonal jumps down and back in the middle. The jumps add a
feeling of power to the melody. Significantly, they occur on the words
"God Omni[potent]." Further, each jump is a full octave, a Baroque
convention signifying everything, "all." God is omnipotent, all-
powerful. (See Example 12 below.)

EXAMPLE 12

Handel may have taken the melody, minus the octave jumps,
from a Lutheran chorale he would have known from his youth, the
second and fifth phrases of Phillip Nicolai's "Wie schön leuchtet der
Morgenstern" ("How brightly shines the Morning Star"). Reference to
that chorale, particularly the fifth phrase, is appropriate here. As noted
above, this scene in *Messiah* is a coronation, and the context of its text
(Rev. 19:6) is the marriage of the Lamb. The words of the fifth phrase
of Nicolai's chorale refers to Jesus as "Mein König und mein
Bräutigam" ("My King and my Bridegroom"), conflate the images of
coronation ("my King") and marriage ("my Bridegroom").

Four more of the quick hallelujahs immediately follow the unison
statement of "for the Lord God Omnipotent reigneth," now with the
trumpets joining for the first time. Then the whole process is repeated
in a different key. But Handel is not yet done with the "God Omnipotent" melody. He states it four more times in succession, now accompanied by the quick hallelujahs tossed from part to part, the orchestra

joining in the jubilation. Two echoes of the quick hallelujah motive in the orchestra bring this section to an end.

For the next section of text Handel again used a hymn-like melody. The choir, with orchestra doubling, sings the first phrase in hymn-like four-part harmony in a low range: "The Kingdom of this world." The cadence repeats for "is become," and then without warning, both the choir and the orchestra, including the trumpets, jump to a much higher range for "the Kingdom of our Lord and of His Christ."

Again, Handel may have borrowed from a Nicolai chorale, this time the seventh and eighth phrases of "Wachet auf, ruft uns die Stimme" (Wake, Awake, for Night Is Flying). (See Example 13 below.)

EXAMPLE 13

Although this musical phrase is very commonplace — it simply goes down the lower five notes of the scale — it is likely that Handel consciously borrowed it, because a few measures later the basses begin the next section singing "and He shall reign forever and ever" to a theme that is remarkably similar to the third, sixth, and eleventh phrases of "Wachet auf." (See Example 14 on p. 138.) And this musical phrase is very distinctive, so the strong similarities between it and the "and He shall reign" theme can hardly be coincidental.

"Wachet auf," like "Wie schön leuchtet," refers to marriage. The two musical phrases that Handel likely borrowed from it are for the following lines of text: "Wohl auf, der Bräutgam kommt" ("Rise up, the Bridegroom comes") and "Ihr müsset ihm entgegen gehn!" ("You must go out to meet him!") Although the text of the chorus at this point

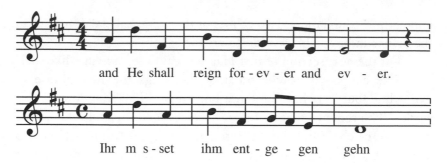

EXAMPLE 14

comes from Revelation 11, texts from Revelation 19 surround it. Likely, Handel was reading it all in the context of Revelation 19, conflating the two images of coronation and marriage. Christ as King and Christ as Bridegroom are two of the Bible's ways of expressing the mystery of the relationship of Christ and his church.

The theme for "and He shall reign for ever and ever" becomes the theme for a short fugal section. After it has been stated in all four voice parts, the sopranos and altos launch into the final bit of text, "King of Kings and Lord of Lords," intoned on a single note, but repeated several times at successively higher pitches. The trumpet joins the sopranos in the rising sequence, and all the while the lower voices and the strings are singing and playing the quick hallelujah motive: "forever and ever, Hallelujah, Hallelujah!"

The whole passage reaches a thrilling climax, but there is more to come:

- a fugal episode in which we hear the "He shall reign" theme two more times, now joined by a lively counter-melody;
- the tenors sing the "King of Kings" motive with the quick hallelujah motive dancing around it;
- the basses sing the "He shall reign" theme with a strong chordal accompaniment above them;
- the basses and sopranos declaim "King of Kings, and Lord of Lords" with powerful upward leaps while the middle voices, trumpets, and tympani sing and play those words to music very

much like "Lift up your heads, O ye gates," and the violins play upward rushing runs;

- all of which leads to one last statement by the basses of the "He shall reign" theme followed just two beats later by the sopranos and trumpet;
- then a final flurry of the quick hallelujah motive repeated eight times on "forever" and "hallelujah";
- a grand pause;
- and a slow, powerful cadence using the "amen" chords:

"HAL-LE _ _ _ _ _ LU _ JAH_____."

Chapter 9

Part the Third

Resurrection of the Dead, Worship of the Lamb

SCENE 1
45. *Aria:* I know that my Redeemer liveth
46. *Chorus:* Since by man came death

SCENE 2
47. *Accompanied recitative:* Behold, I tell you a mystery
48. *Aria:* The trumpet shall sound

SCENE 3
49. Secco *recitative:* Then shall be brought to pass
50. *Duet:* O death, where is thy sting
51. *Chorus:* But thanks be to God
52. *Aria:* If God be for us

SCENE 4
53. *Chorus:* Worthy is the Lamb

Part III is considerably shorter than the previous two parts, and its scenes nearly follow the normal order of recitative-aria-chorus. Even though none of its scenes has exactly the recitative-aria-chorus structure, each of the first three scenes has only one departure from the norm. Scene 1 has no recitative, Scene 2 has no chorus, and Scene 3 has an extra aria after the chorus. Like Part II, Part III ends with a chorus that is a scene unto itself — there a coronation anthem, here an eternal hymn of praise.

Scene 1

45. *Aria:* I know that my Redeemer liveth and that He shall stand at the latter day upon the earth. And tho' worms destroy this body, yet in my flesh shall I see God. For now is Christ risen from the dead, the first fruits of them that sleep (Job 19:25-26, 1 Cor. 15:20).

46. *Chorus:* Since by man came death, by man came also the resurrection of the dead. For as in Adam all die, even so in Christ shall all be made alive (1 Cor. 15:21-21).

Although probably no one would want to forgo hearing "I know that my Redeemer liveth," "The trumpet shall sound," and "Worthy is the Lamb," many have probably wondered why Part III is here at all. After the "Hallelujah Chorus," hasn't the complete story been told? The Messiah has come, has conquered Satan, sin, and death, and has been crowned King of Kings and Lord of Lords, for ever and ever — almost implying that all of the King's people will live happily ever after.

Philip Yancey is one listener who wondered, "What more is needed?"

> I had never really considered the question. . . . But as I glanced at the few paragraphs of libretto remaining . . . I realized what was missing from *Messiah*, Parts 1 and 2. . . . Jesus of Nazareth did not come close to fulfilling the soaring predictions of the prophets. . . . Have peace and good will filled the earth since Jesus' birth?[1]

Obviously they haven't. We still fight wars and hear rumors of wars; we still contend with the ever-present seven deadly sins; and, of course, we all die. How can we say that the Messiah has conquered Satan "when," as Tertullian put it, "even his flies still crawl all over us"?

The answer is this: although the victory has been won and its results are certain, the results have not yet been fully realized. As Yancey put it, "The Incarnation did not usher in the end of history — only the beginning of the end."[2] The Kingdom has already come, but at the same time it has not yet come. Holding onto the "already" aspect of the Kingdom in the face of all that says "not yet" requires faith. The central tenet of that faith is Christ's resurrection. As Paul wrote in 1 Corinthians 15, the chapter from which most of the text of Part III was taken, "And if Christ be not raised, your faith is vain. . . . If in this life only we have hope in Christ, we are of all men most miserable. But now is Christ risen from the dead, and become the firstfruits of them that slept" (1 Cor. 15:17-20).

So Part III begins with a profession of faith in the resurrection of Jesus and in our own resurrection. Appropriately, the profession comes from Job,

> that tragic figure who clung stubbornly to faith amid circumstances that called for bleak despair. "I know that my Redeemer liveth, and that He shall stand at the latter day upon the earth," the soprano sings out. Overwhelmed by personal tragedy, with scant evidence of a sovereign God, Job still managed to believe — and, Handel implies, so should we.[3]

The violins open the aria with a lovely introduction that features two significant melodic ideas. The first is the upward leap of a fourth with which the piece begins. It is an interval that expresses confidence — here a quiet, well-assured confidence. With one exception it will serve as the only interval to which the words "I know" are sung. The second melodic idea is a low, quiet, oscillating figure that depicts peaceful rest. It becomes prominent during the second and third parts of the aria at the texts "And tho' worms destroy this body" and "the first fruits of them that sleep." The climax of the piece is reached near the end on "for now is Christ risen," the one line of text that lends itself to literal word-painting. Handel didn't miss the opportunity. The melody starts low and ascends up the scale for more than an octave, reaching a high G$\sharp$ on "risen."

The words of Paul in this aria, "For now is Christ risen from the dead, the first fruits of them that sleep," which join Job's confession in the Burial Service in the Book of Common Prayer, form a direct link to the explanatory chorus that follows: "Since by man came death, by man came also the resurrection of the dead. For as in Adam all die, even so in Christ shall all be made alive." As an expression of personal faith, "I know that my Redeemer liveth" is appropriately sung by a soloist; as a doctrinal explanation about the universality of death through Adam and the universal availability of life through Christ, "Since by man came death" is appropriately sung by the choir.

The text dealing with death through Adam and life through Christ gave Handel an ideal opportunity for musical contrast — another opportunity he would not pass up.

"Since by man came death"	*"by man came also the resurrection"*
grave (slow)	allegro (fast)
long notes	short notes
(halves, quarters, wholes)	(quarters and mostly eighths)
minor	major
dissonant	consonant
chromatic	diatonic
a cappella	choir and orchestra

The significance of having the "death" section sung a cappella might be lost on our ears. We might recognize that the a cappella sound is unique to *Messiah* — it is the only place where the choir is unaccompanied — but to us that is just a pleasing, well-blended sound that we have heard in countless other choral pieces. But to Handel's listeners the a cappella sound was unique not only to *Messiah* but to most of the music they had ever heard. Almost all Baroque choral music has at least a basso continuo accompaniment. So with no instruments at all, something essential was missing; this music sounded empty, even disembodied, compared to the full-bodied sound of the voices with accompanying instruments. Without basso continuo the music would also lack a foundation, the bottom having literally fallen out — a good analogy for the human condition.

Scene 2

47. *Accompanied recitative:* Behold, I tell you a mystery; we shall not all sleep, but we shall all be chang'd, in a moment, in the twinkling of an eye, at the last trumpet (1 Cor. 15:51-52).

48. *Aria:* The trumpet shall sound, and the dead shall be raised, incorruptible, and we shall be chang'd. For this corruptible must put on incorruption, and this mortal must put on immortality (1 Cor. 15:52-53).

Since the texts of Scene 2 continue Paul's discourse on the resurrection of the dead, it might seem that they should be included in Scene 1. To be sure there is continuity, but the text shifts from reflection on the parallelism between death through the man Adam and life through the man Christ to a dramatic vision of the trumpet sounding at the resurrection of the dead to life immortal on the Day of Judgment.

The accompanied recitative that opens the scene is a gem. Its musical-rhetorical gestures perfectly suit the text and lead beautifully into the aria. The opening notes the bass sings, accompanied by a sustained "wash of string sound," subtly anticipate the opening notes of the aria — simply an ascent through the notes of the D major chord (D-F♯-A-D), the notes the natural, valveless trumpets of Handel's day could play. Of course, the rhythm is different, and the aura of suspense created by the quiet "wash of string sound" in the recitative is absent from the aria. The harmony for both is perfectly natural at the start, and in the aria it stays that way. But in the recitative, when the bass reaches the top note, the "home" note or goal of his rising melodic line, instead of sounding like a secure arrival, a subtle change of chord magically opens up a new world on the word "mystery." Then we are told that "we shall all be chang'd," and that it will happen "in a moment, in the twinkling of an eye" (listen to the sudden quickening of pace), "at the last trumpet" (listen to the wash of string sound give way to trumpet-like fanfares).

Little needs to be said about the aria. Every aspect of the music — key, harmony, rhythm, melody — is tailored to showcase the valveless, natural trumpet used in Handel's time. But note, also, that the long melismas in the bass solo always fall on the word "chang'd." Obviously, Handel wanted to emphasize that, but he put little emphasis on *what* we'll be changed into. The words tell us "the dead shall be rais'd incorruptible," but little in the music calls that to our attention, which is riveted on the sounding of the trumpet.

What will change is emphasized in the second part of the aria. Changes in the music allow the words to be heard without distraction and promote contemplation of the mystery: "For this corruptible must put on incorruption, and this mortal must put on immortality."

> As the text in the middle part again passes over to a more contemplative attitude . . . the music also changes character. The powerful and brilliant disappear. The orchestra falls silent, save for a continuo group, and thus the strong rhythmical marking and contrast also disappears. And as opposed to the tendency of the main part towards strong melodic ascents, the middle part has a definite tendency towards smoothly descending melodic phrases; moreover, it is consistently minor. Thus there is a fine contrast between the two parts, well justified by the direct vision and subsequent contemplation of the text.[4]

After the contemplative second part, the dramatic, trumpet-centered first part returns.

Performed in its entirety this is a very long aria, second in length only to "He was despised." Unfortunately, that leads to many performances in which the theologically and devotionally important middle part is left out.

Scene 3

49. Secco *recitative:* Then shall be brought to pass the saying that is written, death is swallow'd up in victory (1 Cor. 15:54).

50. *Duet:* O Death, where is thy sting, O grave, where is thy victory? The sting of death is sin, and the strength of sin is the law (1 Cor. 15:55-56).

51. *Chorus:* But thanks be to God, who giveth us the victory through our Lord Jesus Christ! (1 Cor. 15:57).

52. *Aria:* If God be for us, who can be against us? Who shall lay anything to the charge of God's elect? It is God that justifieth, who is he that condemneth? It is Christ that died, yea rather, that is risen again, who is at the right hand of God, who maketh intercession for us (Rom. 8:31, 33-34).

Paul's discourse on the resurrection of the dead continues, but the new scene marks another change in focus. The contemplation of the mystery and the thrill of the last trumpet give way to a progression of events: first a duet mocking death ("Death, where is thy sting?"); then a choral expression of gratitude; and finally words (now from Romans) that give us a foundation for living in hope during the "not yet" time.

A simple recitative leads into the scene, followed by a duet in which the singers enjoy tossing their taunts at death and the grave back and forth above a light, bouncing bass line. A short second section toward the end brings new thematic material and a more serious tone for the words "the sting of death is sin, and the strength of sin is the law." As in "Why do the nations," Handel here sets us up to expect a da capo aria (A-B-A form), but as he did there, instead of returning to the beginning, he brings in the choir. It enters without break and begins with the same melody as the first part of the duet: "O death, death, where is thy sting" becomes "But thanks, thanks, thanks be to God." The basses sing the melody while the other voices sing in block chords above them. Then new thematic material is introduced for the rest of the text — "who giveth us the victory through our Lord Jesus Christ." The two parts of the text, each with its own thematic material, alternate throughout the chorus in a variety of fugal, antiphonal, and homophonic textures that reach a climax in the strong cadential phrase, "through our Lord Jesus Christ."

After this choral celebration of victory, many are ready for a final chorus of praise. That being the case, and the evening's entertainment having already gone on for more than two hours, the final aria, "If God be for us," is often omitted. But it is the most comforting text in *Mes-*

siah for our day-to-day existence in the "not yet" time. Though Satan, sin, and death have already been conquered, they still ravage the world. But Christ "is at the right hand of God," and it is he "who makes intercession for us."

The text offers nothing dramatic or highly affective. It is what Burrows calls a "neutral" text, and therefore the aria is "music-led" as opposed to "text-led."[5] The music that "leads" this comforting text is a gracefully flowing larghetto, an example of Handel's lovely lyricism.

Scene 4

53. *Chorus:* Worthy is the Lamb that was slain, and hath redeemed us to God by His blood, to receive power, and riches, and wisdom, and strength, and honour, and glory and blessing. Blessing and honour, glory and pow'r be unto Him that sitteth upon the throne and unto the Lamb for ever and ever. Amen (Rev. 5:12, 9, 13-14).

The final scene takes us to the throne room in heaven. To understand the full meaning of this chorus (actually a triptych of choruses) we need to know the context of the words. In Revelation 4 John sees twenty-four elders seated on thrones surrounding the throne of God, at the sides of which stand four living creatures — a lion, an ox, a man, and an eagle. They sing: "Holy, holy, holy, Lord God Almighty, which was, and is, and is to come" (Rev. 4:8). Their hymn is augmented by the twenty-four elders who "fall down before him that sat on the throne . . . and cast their crowns before the throne, saying, Thou art worthy, O Lord, to receive glory and honour and power: for thou hast created all things, and by thy pleasure they are and were created" (Rev. 4:10-11).

God holds a scroll in his right hand, a symbol of authority. The scroll, as Matthew Henry explains, contains "the whole Mystery of God's Counsel and Conduct"[6] — words that recall Jennens's motto for *Messiah*. But "no one in heaven or on earth or under the earth was able to open the scroll or to look into it." So John weeps, but he is comforted when one of the elders says, "Weep not: behold, the Lion of the Tribe of Judah, the Root of David, hath prevailed to open the book, and to loose its seven seals" (Rev. 5:5).

Henry comments:

> The Apostle was comforted, and encouraged to hope this sealed Book should yet be opened. Here observe . . . who it was that would do the thing; the Lord Jesus Christ, called, *the Lion of the Tribe of Judah,* according to his Divine Nature . . . and, *the Root of David,* according to his Divine Nature, tho' Branch of *David,* according to the Flesh. He who . . . bears the Office of Mediator between God and Man, is fit and worthy to open and execute all the Counsels of God towards Men . . . and he will do it, to the Consolation and Joy of all his People.[7]

John looks toward the Lion, and there "stood a Lamb standing as it had been slain" (Rev. 5:6).

> Before he is called *a Lyon;* here he appears *as a Lamb slain:* He is a Lyon to conquer Satan, a Lamb to satisfy the Justice of God. He appears with the Marks of his Sufferings upon him, to shew that he intercedes in Heaven, in the virtue of his Satisfaction.[8]

The Lamb takes the scroll, and the four living creatures and the twenty-four elders fall down before the Lamb and sing a new song: "Worthy art thou to take the book, and to open the seals thereof: for thou wast slain, and hast redeemed us to God by thy blood out of every kindred, and tongue, and people, and nation; and hast made us unto our God kings and priests; and we shall reign on the earth" (Rev. 5:9).

But this is not yet the climax. "Ten thousand times ten thousand and thousands of thousands" of angels join the four living creatures and elders, singing: "Worthy is the Lamb that was slain, to receive power, and riches, and wisdom, and strength, and honour, and glory, and blessing" (Rev. 5:12).

The crescendo continues as "every creature which is in heaven, and on earth, and under the earth, and such as are in the sea, and all that are in them" continue the song: "Blessing, and honour, and glory, and power, be unto him that sitteth upon the throne, and unto the Lamb forever and ever." And the living creatures say, "Amen!" and the elders fall down and worship.

To say that it is a tall order to compose the music for this final chorus of *Messiah* would be a gross understatement. Suffice it to say that few could have succeeded as well as Handel did. He made of it a choral triptych like the one he made for the suffering of the Lamb in Part II. Both triptychs begin with a pair of choruses that could be called a prelude and fugue. (Here "Worthy is the Lamb" is the prelude, "Blessing and honor, glory and pow'r" is the fugue.) The third parts of the triptychs, however, are very different from each other — "All we like sheep" is light and airy like the secular duet from which it was derived; "Amen" is a highly sophisticated fugue. But each flows smoothly from its predecessors, both textually and musically.

Handel's three-part structure for "Worthy is the Lamb" corresponds to the three parts of the hymn as presented in Revelation. The first part, "Worthy is the Lamb," began when "ten thousand times ten thousand and thousands of thousands" of angels joined the four creatures and the twenty-four elders who had been singing the earlier hymns in chapters 4 and 5. Then for the next section, "Blessing and honor, glory and power," the choir was joined by "every creature in heaven and on earth and under the earth and in the sea." The third section, "Amen," was sung by the four creatures. Handel's divisions are the same, but the "performers" don't correspond. All three of his sections employ the full orchestra and choir, so in the literal sense no voices are added to the performing forces for the second section when "every creature" joins. It would have been possible, of course, to reduce the "Amen" to a quartet representing the four living creatures, but for obvious reasons, that wouldn't make a satisfactory ending for the oratorio. Nevertheless, as we shall see, Handel's music does suggest something of the changes in performers indicated in Revelation 5.

The first chorus of the triptych consists of two contrasting parts that alternate A-B-A-B ("A" consisting of the first part of the text — "Worthy is the Lamb . . ." — and "B" consisting of the second — "to receive power . . ."). Both are entirely homophonic, but "A" is slow and broad and "B" is faster. Both parts employ the full orchestra with the choir (that is, Handel didn't save any performers to represent the addition of "every creature" in the second chorus). However, the texture displays some variety that suggests the addition of "every creature." Since neither timpani nor valveless trumpets were capable of playing all the notes needed to fit with the choir's harmonies, they drop out occasionally. The first "A" section is without timpani, and the second is without both timpani and trumpets. Both, however, can play the "B" sections. With both trumpets and timpani available in the "B" sections, the violins were free to break away from the choir and do something independent. Handel gave them downward rushing scales that add to the fullness and brilliance of the section.

The second chorus ("Blessing and honor") is a fugue, and since fugues begin with one voice part, Handel could not have begun it with added performers to represent "every creature" even if he had held some in reserve for this moment. What the fugue form allowed him to do instead was to start small and continually build. So even though he couldn't follow the performance descriptions in Revelation literally, he could, in this fugue, represent very impressively the gradual swelling of the heavenly choir.

The chorus starts with a typical fugal exposition. Each voice part, doubled by stringed instruments, enters with the theme, one after another until all are singing. Next comes a stretto in which new entrances of the theme occur in close succession, giving the impression of a rapid piling up of voices. The string parts double the voices an octave higher to enhance this impression. Soon the violins break free from the choir and add their own virtuosic sixteenth-note figures to the texture while the voices sing the theme not in succession but simultaneously. Trumpets join the voices, at first in strong, low unisons. Then they climb higher with fanfare-like motives until they join the sopranos and altos an octave above them. Finally all instruments and voices join together in a thrilling climax, singing and playing "for ever and ever, for ever and ever, for ever and ever . . ." until they reach a powerful, slow half-cadence that sets up another fugue on "Amen!"

The theme of the "Amen" fugue is noteworthy. It ascends, with a couple of minor detours, from its lowest note to its final note an octave

A page from Handel's autograph score of the "Amen" Chorus. The British Library, London, England.

above its starting point. A self-contained melody that ends on its highest note is highly unusual. Here, no doubt, it represents the praises offered up to the Lamb.

Unlike the preceding fugue, starting with one voice part (always doubled by strings) and building up one voice at a time can easily be construed as following the performance description in Revelation — the four successive entrances of the theme representing the four living creatures. That impression continues after all four voice parts have entered because the same thing starts to happen again, this time with the instruments alone. The first violins play the fugue theme and the second violins follow. As expected, a third entrance of the theme follows, but in a totally surprising way. Instead of the violas or cellos providing the next entrance in what we assume to be an instrumental exposition, the bass voices have the theme. And they're not alone. The whole choir and orchestra come in, providing rich chordal harmony above the theme in the basses. Undaunted by this outburst, the first and second violins continue their duet. But the same outburst (in a different key) occurs just two measures later. "Every living creature" cannot be silent and leave the eternal "Amen" for the four living creatures alone. So from now until the end everybody will participate. We'll no longer hear the theme in its entirety. Instead its opening five notes will dominate throughout — ascending and descending with various extensions, moving from part to part in various combinations, usually in exciting stretti with one part after another piling up — until they all reach a final grand pause, after which there is one last powerful Handelian cadence:

"A - - - MEN————, A - - - MEN————!"

Glossary

Antiphony (adj. **antiphonal**): Music performed alternately by two or more groups of performers.

Aria: A piece for solo voice(s), usually part of a larger work (such as an opera, oratorio, or cantata), and typically in a lyrical or virtuosic style with much repetition of words and phrases. In Baroque arias the vocal soloist might be accompanied by **basso continuo** only. More typically there will also be one or more and instruments. The function of arias in opera is to portray the affect (or emotion) generated by the dialogue and action that took place in the preceding **recitative**. (Compare **recitative**; see also **da capo**.)

Arioso: (See **recitative**.)

Basso continuo: A type of accompaniment that provides the foundation of most Baroque music. It consists of a bass line with figures that indicate the harmony. It is typically performed on two types of instruments — bass instruments (such as cello, bassoon) to play the bass line, and chordal instruments (such as harpsichord, organ, lute) to improvise the harmonies above the bass line.

Cadence (adj. **cadential**): The moment of resolution at the end of a musical phrase, usually achieved by standard melodic and/or harmonic formulas. Cadences are analogous to punctuation marks. Like them they have varying degrees of finality.

Castrato (pl. **castrati**): An adult male singer whose soprano or alto range was preserved by castration.

Chord: Three or more notes sounding simultaneously. In traditional harmony chords are built out of notes an interval of a third apart (for example, C-E-G) and have well-defined functional relationships to each other that give a series of chords a sense of progression toward a goal.

Chromatic: (See **diatonic**.)

Consonance (adj. **consonant**): A relative term that describes a stable, well-blended, sweet-sounding relationship between tones. (See also **dissonance**.)

Da capo: A term that tells a performer to repeat "from the head" (that is, go back to the beginning) and continue until there is a sign indicating the end. Many **arias** from the Baroque period are in da capo form. They have two main sections, A-B. At the end of the B section the words "da capo" (or simply d.c.) instruct the performer to return to the beginning and repeat the A section. The result is a three-part (or da capo) form — A-B-A.

Diatonic: Music that melodically and/or harmonically mainly employs the normal, unaltered notes of the scale (or key) on which it is based (e.g., C-D-E-F-G-A-B). **Chromatic** music employs many or all of the altered notes as well (for example, C♯, E♭, G♯, etc.). Increased chromaticism makes music more unstable and intense.

Dissonance (adj. **dissonant**): A relative term that describes an unstable, clashing, harsh-sounding relationship between tones. (See also **consonance**.)

Dotted rhythm: A jerky rhythm consisting of a long note followed by a short note (or group of notes). The long one is at least three times the length of the short one. At a slow to moderate tempo, dotted rhythms give music a stately, ceremonial character associated with the pomp and ceremony of a royal procession. At a fast tempo they convey a vicious affect often associated with scourging.

Double: As a verb "double" refers to an instrument playing the same part as a voice or another instrument, for example, an oboe doubling the sopranos and/or the violins.

Drone: A long-held note, usually in the bass, often intended to imitate the sound of a bagpipe.

Fugue (adj. **fugal**)/**double fugue/stretto**: A type of composition based on a theme (called the subject). It typically begins with an exposition in which the subject is presented alone at the beginning and then enters successively in the other parts. Throughout the piece the subject appears periodically in different parts, sometimes with overlapping entrances called **stretto**. A **double fugue** is a fugue with two subjects.

Grand pause: All the voices and instruments fall silent for a short, unmeasured length of time.

Homophonic: A musical **texture** consisting of a melody with accompaniment, as opposed, for example, to a texture in which all the parts are more or less equal in melodic and rhythmic importance.

Interval: The difference in **pitch** between two tones.

Libretto: Literally "little book." The text of a vocal piece of music such as an opera, oratorio, or cantata. A librettist is the author of a libretto.

Masque: A type of entertainment consisting of costumes (typically including masks), scenery, dance, music, and poetry (but not dramatic dialogue). The subject matter is usually mythological or allegorical. Masques were popular among the aristocracy in England during the sixteenth and seventeenth centuries.

Octave: An **interval** between two pitches that are so **consonant** with each other that they sound almost identical, even though one is considerably higher than the other. The perfect **consonance** between the two pitches is due to the fact that the frequency of the higher pitch is twice that of the lower one.

Patent theater: A theater in England that was granted a patent to perform serious drama. Such performances had been banned under the Commonwealth but were restored by Charles II in 1660 during the English Restoration.

Pitch: The relative highness or lowness of a tone.

Recitative — secco, accompanied, arioso: A piece for solo voice(s) within a larger composition such as an opera, oratorio, or cantata. The style is declamatory — recitation-like. Words are not usually repeated, there is usually just one note per syllable, and the rhythms and melodic inflections are close to those of oratorical speaking. The function of recitatives in opera is to carry the dialogue and advance the dramatic action. (Compare **aria**.) Some, called **secco recitatives**, have only a **basso continuo** accompaniment. Others, called **accompanied recitatives**, include additional instruments. Some, called **ariosos**, tend toward **arias** in style by virtue of having some repeated words and phrases as well as a more lyrical style.

Sequence: Successive repetitions of a melodic motive or phrase at regularly higher or lower pitch levels.

Stile antico: Literally "old (or ancient) style." A style of Baroque music that more or less imitates Renaissance style. Typically associated with church style *(stile ecclesiasticus)* as opposed to theatrical style.

Stile concitato: Agitated, angry, or warlike style. Mainly characterized by rapid, repeated sixteenth notes over static or simple, slow-changing harmonies.

Stile ecclesiasticus: (See *stile antico.*)

Stile rappresentativo: Literally "representative style." A style of solo singing developed in early opera. It is characterized by a great deal of freedom and irregularity in rhythm and phrasing, thus "representing" the dramatic speech of an orator or actor.

Stretto: (See **fugue.**)

Texture: By analogy with textiles, texture in music refers to the "weave" of the different musical "threads." The most basic aspects of musical texture are the number of parts and how they are related to each other in range, rhythmic activity, melodic shape, and function.

Turba **chorus:** Literally "crowd chorus." The short, dramatic choruses in Passions that set the words in the narrative that are spoken by groups of people (the disciples, the chief priests and scribes, the soldiers, the crowd, and so on).

Unison: Tones of the same **pitch** sounded together are said to be "in unison" (literally "one sound"). Sometimes the phrase is expanded to include one or more **octaves**, as when a choir is said to sing in unison even though the men and women are singing an octave apart.

Notes

Notes to the Preface

1. Wilson Follett, *Modern American Usage: A Guide* (Grosset and Dunlap, Inc., 1970), p. 71.

2. C. S. Lewis, *A Preface to Paradise Lost* (New York: Oxford University Press, 1961), p. 1.

Notes to Chapter 1: Oratorio before Handel

1. Winton Dean, *Handel's Dramatic Oratorios and Masques* (New York: Oxford University Press, 1959), p. 3.

2. Quoted from Claude Palisca, *Baroque Music* (Englewood Cliffs, N.J.: Prentice Hall, 1968), pp. 113-114.

3. Howard Smither, *A History of the Oratorio*, vol. 2 (Chapel Hill: University of North Carolina Press, 1977), p. 105.

4. Quoted from Smither, *A History of the Oratorio*, vol. 2, p. 110.

5. Smither, *A History of the Oratorio*, vol. 2, p. 131.

6. Winton Dean and Anthony Hicks, *The New Grove Handel* (New York: W. W. Norton and Co., 1983), p. 21.

Notes to Chapter 2: Handel

1. John Mainwaring, *Memoirs of the Life of the Late George Frederic Handel* (London, 1760), pp. 39-40.

2. Mainwaring, *Memoirs of the Life of Handel*, pp. 40-41.

3. Quoted from Howard Smither, *A History of the Oratorio,* vol. 1 (Chapel Hill: University of North Carolina Press, 1977), p. 265.

4. Mainwaring, *Memoirs of the Life of Handel,* pp. 51-52.

5. Mainwaring, *Memoirs of the Life of Handel,* p. 60.

6. Mainwaring, *Memoirs of the Life of Handel,* pp. 71-72.

7. Donald Jay Grout, *A Short History of Opera* (New York: Columbia University Press, 1965), p. 136.

8. Grout, *A Short History of Opera,* p. 137.

9. John Downs, *Roscius Anglicanus* (London, 1708), p. 48.

10. François Raguenet, *A Comparison Between French and Italian Musick and Opera's. Translated from the French: with some remarks. To which is added A critical discouse upon opera's in England* (London, 1709), p. 67.

11. Joseph Addison, *The Spectator,* vol. 1, ed. G. Gregory Smith (New York: E. P. Dutton and Co., 1907), issue no. 5, 6 March 1711, pp. 17-19.

12. Donald Burrows, *Handel* (New York: Schirmer Books, 1994), p. 78.

13. Quoted from Otto Erich Deutsch, *Handel: A Documentary Biography* (London: Adam and Charles Black, 1955), p. 210.

14. John Arbuthnot, *Miscellaneous Works,* vol. 1 (Glasgow, 1751), pp. 213-214.

15. Addison, *The Spectator,* vol. 1, issue no. 18, 21 March 1711, pp. 55-56.

16. Samuel Johnson, "Life of Hughes," in *The Lives of the English Poets* (Dublin, 1779-1781), vol. 1, p. 532.

17. Johnson, "Life of Gay," in *The Lives of the English Poets,* vol. 3, p. 8.

18. Johnson, "Life of Gay," p. 10.

19. Quoted from Deutsch, *Handel: A Documentary Biography,* pp. 223-224.

20. Quoted from Deutsch, *Handel: A Documentary Biography,* p. 220.

21. Quoted from Deutsch, *Handel: A Documentary Biography,* p. 223.

22. Johnson, "Life of Gay," pp. 10-11.

23. James Boswell, *The Life of Samuel Johnson* (New York: The Modern Library, n.d.), p. 537.

24. Boswell, *The Life of Samuel Johnson,* p. 536.

25. Johnson, "Life of Gay," p. 11.

26. Quoted from Deutsch, *Handel: A Documentary Biography,* p. 285.

27. Quoted from Deutsch, *Handel: A Documentary Biography,* p. 286.

28. Quoted from Deutsch, *Handel: A Documentary Biography,* pp. 288-289.

29. Quoted from Deutsch, *Handel: A Documentary Biography,* p. 292.

30. Charles Burney, *An Account of the Musical Performances in Westminster-Abbey* (London, 1785), pp. 100-101.

31. Richard Luckett, *Handel's Messiah: A Celebration* (New York: Harcourt Brace and Company, 1992), pp. 28-29.

32. Henry Carey, *The Dragon of Wantley: A Burlesque Opera* (London, 1738), pp. iii-iv.

33. Carey, *The Dragon of Wantley,* p. 16.

34. Carey, *The Dragon of Wantley*, p. 19.
35. Carey, *The Dragon of Wantley*, p. 21.
36. Carey, *The Dragon of Wantley*, p. 32.
37. Carey, *The Dragon of Wantley*, p. iv.

Notes to Chapter 3: *Messiah*

1. John Brown, *A Dissertation on the Rise, Union, and Power, the Progressions, Separations, and Corruptions, of Poetry and Music* (London, 1763), p. 218.

2. From a letter to Edward Holdsworth, 10 July 1741. Quoted from Donald Burrows, *Handel: Messiah,* Cambridge Music Handbooks, gen. ed. Julian Rushton (Cambridge: Cambridge University Press, 1991), p. 11.

3. Newman Flower, *George Frideric Handel: His Personality and His Times* (Boston: Houghton Mifflin Company, 1923), p. 251, attributes this to Johnson but without identifying a source. I have encountered it in other places as well, but always without a source.

4. This and the following quotations from Steevens regarding Jennens are from John Nichols, *Literary Anecdotes of the Eighteenth Century,* vol. 3 (London, 1812), pp. 120-126.

5. Ruth Smith, "Handel's English Librettists," in *The Cambridge Companion to Handel,* ed. Donald Burrows (Cambridge: Cambridge University Press, 1997), p. 95.

6. Quoted from Ruth Smith, "The Achievements of Charles Jennens (1700-1773)," *Music and Letters* 70, no. 2 (May 1989): 171.

7. Quoted from Otto Erich Deutsch, *Handel: A Documentary Biography* (London: Adam and Charles Black, 1955), p. 530.

8. Letter dated Dec. 2, 1741. Quoted from Burrows, *Handel: Messiah,* p. 14.

9. Quoted from Deutsch, *Handel: A Documentary Biography,* p. 542.

10. Quoted from Deutsch, *Handel: A Documentary Biography,* p. 545.

11. Quoted from Deutsch, *Handel: A Documentary Biography,* pp. 544-546.

12. Quoted from Burrows, *Handel: Messiah,* p. 20.

13. Quoted from Deutsch, *Handel: A Documentary Biography,* pp. 563-564.

14. Quoted from Deutsch, *Handel: A Documentary Biography,* pp. 565-566.

15. Quoted from Deutsch, *Handel: A Documentary Biography,* p. 568.

16. Quoted from Deutsch, *Handel: A Documentary Biography,* p. 848.

17. Quoted from Burrows, *Handel: Messiah,* p. 24.

18. Quoted from Burrows, *Handel: Messiah,* p. 29.

19. Quoted from Burrows, *Handel: Messiah,* p. 35.

20. Quoted from Burrows, *Handel: Messiah,* p. 32.

21. Quoted from Deutsch, *Handel: A Documentary Biography,* p. 669.

22. Quoted from Deutsch, *Handel: A Documentary Biography,* pp. 477-478.

23. Charles Burney, *An Account of the Musical Performances in Westminster-Abbey* (London, 1785), pp. vi-vii.

24. Burney, *An Account of the Musical Performances in Westminster-Abbey*, p. 27.

25. Marian Van Til, *George Frideric Handel: A Music Lover's Guide* (Youngstown, N.Y.: WordPower Publishing, 2007), pp. 9 and 11.

26. Quoted from Deutsch, *Handel: A Documentary Biography*, p. 731.

27. See Deutsch, *Handel: A Documentary Biography*, pp. 804-806.

28. Burney, *An Account of the Musical Performances in Westminster-Abbey*, p. 31.

29. Quoted from Deutsch, *Handel: A Documentary Biography*, pp. 818-819.

30. Quoted from Deutsch, *Handel: A Documentary Biography*, p. 814.

31. Richard Taruskin, *Music in the Seventeenth and Eighteenth Centuries*, The Oxford History of Western Music, vol. 2 (Oxford: Oxford University Press, 2010), p. 326.

32. Richard Luckett, *Handel's Messiah: A Celebration* (New York: Harcourt Brace and Company, 1992), p. 208.

33. Nichols, *Literary Anecdotes of the Eighteenth Century*, vol. 3, p. 126.

34. Chris Goddard, "The Handel Festivals and Crystal Palace." On line at: www.webarian.co.uk/crystalpalace107.html (accessed 27 November 2004).

35. Quoted from Karl Geiringer, *Haydn: A Creative Life in Music* (Garden City, N.Y.: Doubleday, 1963), pp. 119-120.

36. Quoted from and translated by Vernon Gotwals, *Haydn: Two Contemporary Portraits* (Madison: University of Wisconsin Press, 1968), p. 235.

37. Quoted from Howard Smither, *A History of the Oratorio*, vol. 4 (Chapel Hill: University of North Carolina Press, 2000), p. 282.

38. George Bernard Shaw, *Shaw's Music*, vol. 3, ed. Dan H. Laurence (New York: Dodd, Mead and Company, 1981), pp. 640-641.

39. George Bernard Shaw, *Shaw on Music*, ed. Eric Bentley (Garden City, N.Y.: Doubleday, 1955), pp. 245-246.

40. Shaw, *Shaw's Music*, pp. 638-639.

41. Quoted from Burrows, *Handel: Messiah*, p. 52.

Notes to Chapter 4: To Teach and Delight

1. Quoted from Otto Erich Deutsch, *Handel: A Documentary Biography* (London: Adam and Charles Black, 1955), p. 292.

2. Quoted from Deutsch, *Handel: A Documentary Biography*, pp. 544-545.

3. In a letter to an unknown addressee. Quoted from Donald Burrows, *Handel: Messiah*, Cambridge Music Handbooks, gen. ed. Julian Rushton (Cambridge: Cambridge University Press, 1991), p. 35.

4. Howard Smither, *A History of the Oratorio,* vol. 2 (Chapel Hill: University of North Carolina Press, 1977), p. 197.

5. Jens Peter Larsen, *Handel's Messiah: Origins, Composition, Sources* (New York: W. W. Norton and Co., 1957), p. 16.

6. Quoted from Deutsch, *Handel: A Documentary Biography,* p. 855.

7. Quoted from Deutsch, *Handel: A Documentary Biography,* p. 854.

8. Samuel Johnson, "Life of Gay," in *The Lives of the English Poets* (Dublin, 1779-1781), vol. 3, p. 11.

9. Quoted from Brian Vickers, *English Renaissance Literary Criticism* (Oxford: Oxford University Press, 1999), p. 366.

10. M. H. Abrams, *The Mirror and the Lamp* (New York: Oxford University Press, 1971), p. 16.

11. Abrams, *The Mirror and the Lamp,* pp. 14-15.

12. Quoted from Vickers, *English Renaissance Literary Criticism,* p. 568.

13. Quoted from Vickers, *English Renaissance Literary Criticism,* pp. 469-470.

14. Johann Mattheson, *Der vollkommene Capellmeister,* trans. Ernest C. Harriss (Ann Arbor: UMI Research Press, 1981), p. 104; my emphasis.

15. Quoted from Vickers, *English Renaissance Literary Criticism,* p. 71.

16. Quoted from Piero Weiss and Richard Taruskin, *Music in the Western World: A History in Documents* (New York: Schirmer Books, 1984), p. 303.

17. Quoted from Vickers, *English Renaissance Literary Criticism,* p. 358.

18. James Beattie, *Essays on Poetry and Music,* 3rd ed. (London, 1779), p. 10.

19. Roger Kimball, "'Art' Isn't Exempt from Moral Criticism," *Wall Street Journal,* 24 September 1999, p. A14.

20. Wayne C. Booth, *The Company We Keep: An Ethics of Fiction* (Berkeley: University of California Press, 1988), p. 5.

21. Quoted from Burrows, *Handel: Messiah,* p. 20.

Notes to Chapter 5: *Messiah* versus Deism

1. Wayne C. Booth, *The Company We Keep: An Ethics of Fiction* (Berkeley: University of California Press, 1988), p. 4.

2. Richard Taruskin, *Music in the Seventeenth and Eighteenth Centuries,* The Oxford History of Western Music, vol. 2 (Oxford: Oxford University Press, 2010), p. 34.

3. Taruskin, *Music in the Seventeenth and Eighteenth Centuries,* p. 151.

4. Newburgh Hamilton, quoted in Ruth Smith, *Handel's Oratorios and Eighteenth-Century Thought* (Cambridge: Cambridge University Press, 1995), p. 22.

5. Smith, *Handel's Oratorios and Eighteenth-Century Thought,* p. 343.

6. Richard Kidder, *A Demonstration of the Messias. In Which The Truth of the*

Christian Religion Is Proved, against all the Enemies thereof; But especially against the Jews. In three parts (London, 1726), p. ii.

7. Smith, *Handel's Oratorios and Eighteenth-Century Thought*, p. 144.

8. Smith, *Handel's Oratorios and Eighteenth-Century Thought*, p. 150.

9. Kidder, *A Demonstration of the Messias*, p. i.

10. Kidder, *A Demonstration of the Messias*, p. 203.

11. Kidder, *A Demonstration of the Messias*, p. ii.

12. Smith, *Handel's Oratorios and Eighteenth-Century Thought*, p. 151.

13. Quoted from Smith, *Handel's Oratorios and Eighteenth-Century Thought*, p. 151.

14. Ruth Smith, "The Achievements of Charles Jennens (1700-1773)," *Music and Letters* 70, no. 2 (May 1989): 181.

Notes to Chapter 6: Before We Begin

1. Quoted from Donald Burrows, *Handel: Messiah*, Cambridge Music Handbooks, gen. ed. Julian Rushton (Cambridge: Cambridge University Press, 1991), p. 16.

2. Alexander Pope, "Messiah: A Sacred Eclogue in Imitation of Virgil's 'Pollio'" (1712), ll. 7-10.

3. Michael Marissen has recently discovered that one of the sources of Jennens's emendations of the standard King James and Book of Common Prayer translations came from Hammond. See his "Rejoicing against Judaism in Handel's *Messiah*," *The Journal of Musicology* 24, no. 2 (Spring 2007): 167-194.

4. Henry Hammond, *A Paraphrase and Annotations Upon All the Books of the New Testament* (London, 1659), p. 695.

5. Hammond, *A Paraphrase and Annotations Upon all the Books of the New Testament*, p. 692.

Notes to Chapter 7: Part the First

1. Roger A. Bullard, *Messiah: The Gospel according to Handel's Oratorio* (Grand Rapids: Wm. B. Eerdmans Publishing Co., 1993), p. 9.

2. Donald Burrows, *Handel: Messiah*, Cambridge Music Handbooks, gen. ed. Julian Rushton (Cambridge: Cambridge University Press, 1991), p. 68.

3. Bullard, *Messiah: The Gospel according to Handel's Oratorio*, pp. 19-20.

4. Matthew Henry, *An Exposition of All the Books of the Old and New Testament*, vol. 4 (London, 1721), p. 821.

5. Bullard, *Messiah: The Gospel according to Handel's Oratorio*, p. 27.

6. St. Augustine, *Expositions of the Psalms,* vol. 1, trans. Maria Boulding, O.S.B. (Hyde Park, N.Y.: New City Press, 1999), Ps. 32 (2):8.

7. Dietrich Bonhoeffer, *The Cost of Discipleship* (New York: The Macmillan Company, 1963), p. 48.

Notes to Chapter 8: Part the Second

1. Roger A. Bullard, *Messiah: The Gospel according to Handel's Oratorio* (Grand Rapids: Wm. B. Eerdmans Publishing Co., 1993), p. 63.

2. Henry Hammond, *A Paraphrase and Annotations Upon the Books of the Psalms* (London, 1659), p. 340. Following the libretto, I substituted third-person pronouns for first-person pronouns.

3. Bullard, *Messiah: The Gospel according to Handel's Oratorio,* p. 91.

4. Donald Burrows, *Handel: Messiah,* Cambridge Music Handbooks, gen. ed. Julian Rushton (Cambridge: Cambridge University Press, 1991), p. 68.

5. Michael Linton, "America's Messiah," *First Things,* December 1997, p. 17.

6. Jens Peter Larsen, *Handel's Messiah: Origins, Composition, Sources* (New York: W. W. Norton and Co., 1957), p. 150.

7. Bullard, *Messiah: The Gospel according to Handel's Oratorio,* p. 101.

8. Larsen, *Handel's Messiah,* p. 150.

9. Hammond, *A Paraphrase and Annotations Upon the Books of the Psalms,* p. 136.

10. Bullard, *Messiah: The Gospel according to Handel's Oratorio,* p. 103.

11. Bullard, *Messiah: The Gospel according to Handel's Oratorio,* p. 104.

12. Henry Hammond, *A Paraphrase and Annotations Upon All the Books of the New Testament* (London, 1659), p. 622.

13. Hammond, *A Paraphrase and Annotations Upon All the Books of the New Testament,* p. 622.

14. Larsen, *Handel's Messiah,* p. 157.

15. Burrows, *Handel: Messiah,* p. 61.

16. Larsen, *Handel's Messiah,* p. 157.

17. Larsen, *Handel's Messiah,* p. 158.

18. John Tobin, *Handel's Messiah* (New York: St. Martin's Press, 1969), pp. 59-60.

19. Quoted from Burrows, *Handel: Messiah,* p. 11.

20. On Edwards's famous sermon, see George Marsden, *Jonathan Edwards: A Life* (New Haven: Yale University Press, 2003), pp. 221-222. For an illuminating discussion of this oft misunderstood and misrepresented sermon, see pp. 219-224.

21. Marsden, *Jonathan Edwards: A Life,* p. 224.

22. Quoted from Marsden, *Jonathan Edwards: A Life,* p. 223.

23. Ruth Smith, *Handel's Oratorios and Eighteenth-Century Thought* (Cambridge: Cambridge University Press, 1995), p. 357.

24. See Michael Marissen, "Rejoicing against Judaism in Handel's *Messiah*," *The Journal of Musicology* 24, no. 2 (Spring 2007): 167-194. See also his forthcoming book, *Rejoicing Against Judaism: A Forgotten Aspect of Handel's* Messiah.

25. Henry, *An Exposition of the Five Poetical Books of the Old Testament.*

26. Hammond, *A Paraphrase and Annotations Upon the Books of the Psalms,* p. 12.

27. Matthew Henry, *An Exposition of All the Books of the Old and New Testament,* vol. 4 (London, 1721).

Notes to Chapter 9: Part the Third

1. Philip Yancey, *The Bible Jesus Read* (Grand Rapids: Zondervan Publishing Co., 1999), p. 216.

2. Yancey, *The Bible Jesus Read,* p. 216.

3. Yancey, *The Bible Jesus Read,* pp. 216-217.

4. Jens Peter Larsen, *Handel's Messiah: Origins, Composition, Sources* (New York: W. W. Norton and Co., 1957), p. 180.

5. Donald Burrows, *Handel: Messiah,* Cambridge Music Handbooks, gen. ed. Julian Rushton (Cambridge: Cambridge University Press, 1991), p. 61.

6. Matthew Henry, *An Exposition of All the Books of the Old and New Testament,* vol. 6 (London, 1721), p. 694.

7. Henry, *An Exposition of All the Books in the New Testament,* vol. 6, p. 694.

8. Henry, *An Exposition of All the Books in the New Testament,* vol. 6, p. 695.

A List of Works Cited

Primary Sources

Addison, Joseph. *The Spectator.* Volume 1. Ed. G. Gregory Smith. New York: E. P. Dutton and Co., 1907.

Arbuthnot, John. *Miscellaneous Works.* Volume 1. Glasgow, 1751.

Augustine, St. *Expositions of the Psalms.* Volume 1. Trans. Maria Boulding, O.S.B. Hyde Park, N.Y.: New City Press, 1999.

Beattie, James. *Essays on Poetry and Music.* 3rd edition. London, 1779.

Boswell, James. *The Life of Samuel Johnson.* New York: The Modern Library, n.d.

Brown, John. *A Dissertation on the Rise, Union, and Power, the Progressions, Separations, and Corruptions, of Poetry and Music.* London, 1763.

Burney, Charles. *An Account of the Musical Performances in Westminster-Abbey.* London, 1785.

Carey, Henry. *The Dragon of Wantley: A Burlesque Opera.* London, 1738.

Downes, John. *Roscius Anglicanus.* London, 1708.

Hammond, Henry. *A Paraphrase and Annotations Upon All the Books of the New Testament.* London, 1659.

———. *A Paraphrase and Annotations Upon the Books of the Psalms.* London, 1659.

Henry, Matthew. *An Exposition of the Five Poetical Books of the Old Testament.* London, 1710.

———. *An Exposition of All the Books of the Old and New Testament.* Volume 6. London, 1721-1725.

Johnson, Samuel. *The Lives of the English Poets.* Dublin, 1779-1781. "Gay," volume 3, pp. 1-16. "Hughes," volume 1, pp. 531-535.

Kidder, Richard. *A Demonstration of the Messias. In Which The Truth of the*

Christian Religion Is Proved, against all the Enemies thereof; But especially against the Jews. In three parts. London, 1726.

Mainwaring, John. *Memoirs of the Life of the Late George Frederic Handel.* London, 1760.

Mattheson, Johann. *Der vollkommene Capellmeister.* Trans. Ernest C. Harriss. Ann Arbor: UMI Research Press, 1981.

Newton, John. *Messiah: Or, the Scriptural Passages which Form the Subject of the Celebrated Oratorio of Handel.* 1786.

Nichols, John. *Literary Anecdotes of the Eighteenth Century.* Volume 3. London, 1812.

Pope, Alexander. "Messiah: A Sacred Eclogue in Imitation of Virgil's 'Pollio.'" 1712.

Raguenet, François (1660?-1722). *A Comparison Between French and Italian Musick and Opera's. Translated from the French: with some remarks. To which is added A critical discouse upon opera's in England.* London, 1709.

Shaw, George Bernard. *Shaw on Music.* Ed. Eric Bentley. Garden City, N.Y.: Doubleday, 1955.

———. *Shaw's Music.* Volume 3. Ed. Dan H. Laurence. New York: Dodd, Mead and Company, 1981.

Primary Sources — Collections, Anthologies

Deutsch, Otto Erich. *Handel: A Documentary Biography.* London: Adam and Charles Black, 1955.

Vickers, Brian. *English Renaissance Literary Criticism.* Oxford: Oxford University Press, 1999.

Weiss, Piero, and Richard Taruskin. *Music in the Western World: A History in Documents.* New York: Schirmer Books, 1984.

Secondary Sources

Abrams, M. H. *The Mirror and the Lamp.* New York: Oxford University Press, 1971.

Bonhoeffer, Dietrich. *The Cost of Discipleship.* New York: The Macmillan Company, 1963.

Booth, Wayne C. *The Company We Keep: An Ethics of Fiction.* Berkeley: University of California Press, 1988.

Bullard, Roger A. *Messiah: The Gospel according to Handel's Oratorio.* Grand Rapids: Wm. B. Eerdmans Publishing Co., 1993.

Burrows, Donald. *Handel.* New York: Schirmer Books, 1994.

————. *Handel: Messiah.* Cambridge Music Handbooks. Julian Rushton, gen. ed. Cambridge: Cambridge University Press, 1991.

Dean, Winton. *Handel's Dramatic Oratorios and Masques.* New York: Oxford University Press, 1959.

————, with Anthony Hicks. *The New Grove Handel.* New York: W. W. Norton, 1983.

Flower, Newman. *George Frideric Handel: His Personality and His Times.* Boston: Houghton Mifflin Company, 1923.

Follett, Wilson. *Modern American Usage: A Guide.* Grosset and Dunlap, 1970.

Geiringer, Karl. *Haydn: A Creative Life in Music.* Garden City, N.Y.: Doubleday, 1963.

Goddard, Chris. "The 1888 Crystal Palace recordings: The Handel Festivals and Crystal Palace." On line at: www.webrarian.co.uk/crystalpalace/crystal07.html.

Gotwals, Vernon. *Haydn: Two Contemporary Portraits.* Madison: University of Wisconsin Press, 1968.

Grout, Donald Jay. *A Short History of Opera.* New York: Columbia University Press, 1965.

Kimball, Roger. "'Art' Isn't Exempt from Moral Criticism." *Wall Street Journal,* 24 September 1999, p. A14.

Larsen, Jens Peter. *Handel's Messiah: Origins, Composition, Sources.* New York: W. W. Norton, 1957.

Lewis, C. S. *A Preface to Paradise Lost.* New York: Oxford University Press, 1961.

Linton, Michael. "America's Messiah." *First Things,* December 1997, pp. 17-19.

Luckett, Richard. *Handel's Messiah: A Celebration.* New York: Harcourt Brace and Company, 1992.

Marissen, Michael. *Rejoicing against Judaism: A Forgotten Aspect of Handel's Messiah.* Forthcoming.

————. "Rejoicing against Judaism in Handel's *Messiah.*" *The Journal of Musicology* 24, no. 2 (Spring, 2007): 167-194.

Marsden, George. *Jonathan Edwards: A Life.* New Haven: Yale University Press, 2003.

Palisca, Claude. *Baroque Music.* Englewood Cliffs, N.J.: Prentice Hall, 1968.

Smith, Ruth. "The Achievements of Charles Jennens (1700-1773)." *Music and Letters* 70, no. 2 (May 1989): 161-190.

————. "Handel's English Librettists." In *The Cambridge Companion to Handel,* ed. Donald Burrows. Cambridge: Cambridge University Press, 1997.

————. *Handel's Oratorios and Eighteenth-Century Thought.* Cambridge: Cambridge University Press, 1995.

Smither, Howard. *A History of the Oratorio.* Volumes 1, 2, and 4. Chapel Hill: University of North Carolina Press, 1977 and 2000.

Taruskin, Richard. *Music in the Seventeenth and Eighteenth Centuries.* The Oxford History of Western Music, volume 2. Oxford: Oxford University Press, 2010.

Tobin, John. *Handel's Messiah.* New York: St. Martin's Press, 1969.

Van Til, Marian. *George Frideric Handel: A Music Lover's Guide.* Youngstown, N.Y.: WordPower Publishing, 2007.

Yancey, Philip. *The Bible Jesus Read.* Grand Rapids: Zondervan Publishing Co., 1999.

Credits

P. 1   The Bridgeman Art Library International.

P. 5   Photo Credit: Scala/Art Resource, NY.

P. 13   Copyright Gerald Coke Handel Collection, The Foundling Museum.

P. 23   Photo Credit: Cameraphoto Arte Venice / Art Resource, NY.

P. 25   A scene from "The Beggar's Opera" VI (1731). Oil on canvas, 572 x 762 cm. Purchased 1909. Tate Gallery, London, Great Britain. Photo Credit: Tate, London / Art Resource, NY.

P. 31   © City of Westminster Archive Centre, London, UK / The Bridgeman Art Library International.

P. 41   Credit: The Art Archive / Private Collection / Eileen Tweedy.

P. 47   Copyright Gerald Coke Handel Foundation.

P. 52   Reproduced by permission of English Heritage / Heritage-Images.

P. 55   Source: Wikimedia Commons, http://en.wikipedia.org/wiki/File:Commemoration_of_Handel_1784.JPG.

P. 58   Source: Seymour Swets, *Fifty Years of Music at Calvin College* (Grand Rapids: Eerdmans Publishing Company, 1973), p. 112.

P. 60   Photo by Jason Rieffer.

P. 63   Deutsches Historisches Museum, Berlin, Germany / © DHM / The Bridgeman Art Library International.

P. 66   © The Trustees of the British Museum.

P. 79   Private Collection / The Bridgeman Art Library International.

P. 151   © The British Library Board. Shelfmark R.M.20.f.2, 132v.

Index

Abrams, M. H., 68
Act of Settlement, 20
Addison, Joseph, 18-19, 24
Anne, Queen, 19-20
Arciconfraternity del Crocifisso
    (Rome), 7
Arne, Michael, 53
Art, theories of, 67-71
Augustine, St., 104

Bach, Carl Philipp Emanuel, 53
Bach, J. S., 9, 50, 61, 83, 131, 132
Beattie, James, 67, 70, 71
Beggar's Opera, The, 24-28, 54, 67, 73
Blow, John: *Venus and Adonis,* 17
Bonhoeffer, Dietrich, 107
Bononcini, Giovanni, 22; work:
    Camilla, 18
Booth, Wayne, 71
Bordoni, Faustina, 22, 26
Boswell, James, 27
Boyle Lectures. *See* Boyle, Robert
Boyle, Robert, 76
Brockes, Barthold Heinrich, 11
Brown, John, 37
Brydges, James (Duke of Chandos), 20,
    21, 29
Bullard, Roger A., 91, 97, 114, 120
Burial Service. See Croft, William

Burney, Charles, 30, 48-49, 50, 69
Burrows, Donald, 117, 126, 147
Buxtehude, Dieterich, 12

Camilla. See Bononcini, Giovanni
Carey, Henry. *See Dragon of Wantley,*
    The
Carissimi, Giacomo, 7; work: *Jephte,* 7-
    8, 74
Cavalieri, Emilio. *See Rappresentatione*
    di Anima, et di Corpo, 6
Charles II, King, 17
Commonwealth, 16
Corelli, Archangelo, 15
Counter Reformation, 4
Covent Garden, 32, 53, 54
Croft, William: *Burial Service,* 51
Crown and Anchor Tavern, 29
Crystal Palace, 57
Cuzzoni, Francesca, 22, 26

Dafne. See Peri, Jacopo
Dean, Winton, 3, 6, 37
Deism, 72-78
Der blutige und sterbende Jesus. See
    Keiser, Reinhard
Dialogue (musical genre), 11
Dialogue of Job, God, Satan, Job's Wife,

and the Messengers, The. See Hilton, John

Dickens, Charles, 51

Dido and Aeneas. See Purcell, Henry

Dragon of Wantley, The, 32-35

Drury Lane. *See* Theatre Royale in Drury Lane

Dublin, Ireland, 3, 42-44, 48, 53

Duke of Chandos. *See* Brydges, James

Earl of Shaftsbury, 45

Edwards, Jonathan, 131-132

Enlightenment, 75

Eurydice. See Peri, Jacopo

Faustina. *See* Bordoni, Faustina

Foundling Hospital, 47-48, 49, 53

Gay, John. *See Beggar's Opera, The*

George I, King, 16, 19-20, 21, 38

George II, King, 30, 135

George Ludwig, Elector (Hanover). *See* George I, King

Grout, Donald, 16, 17

Guadagni, Guatano, 95-96

Hammond, Henry, 85, 117, 121, 125, 126, 133

Handel and Haydn Society of Boston, 53, 57

Handel, George Frideric: and benefit concerts for charities, 47-49, 56; blindness, 49-50; death, 50-51; education, 12; and his father, 49; in Germany, 12, 14; and *historiae,* 9; illness, 46, 49; in Italy, 14-16; and Lutheran church, 9, 12; musical training, early, 12; and opera, Italian in England, 18-24, 28, 31, 35, 36, 42; and oratorio, origin in England, 28-31; and oratorio, Italian, 8; organist and harpsichordist, 15; problems with star singers, 21-22; purpose of his music, entertainment and devotion, 65-67, 71, 72-75

Handel, George Frideric, works: operas: *Admeto,* 21, 73; *Agrippina,* 15, 16; *Almira,* 12; *Amadigi,* 20; *Deidamia,* 35; *Giulio Cesare,* 21; *Il pastor fido,* 20; *Imeneo,* 35, 36, 42; *Nero,* 12; *Orlando,* 31; *Radamisto,* 21; *Rinaldo,* 18-19, 20, 22; *Rodelinda,* 21, 73; *Roderigo,* 15; *Semele,* 46; *Silla,* 20; *Siroe,* 21; *Tamerlano,* 21; *Teseo,* 20; oratorios: *Athalia,* 35, 74; *Balshazzar,* 74; *Deborah,* 31, 35, 74; *Esther,* 20, 29-31, 35, 42, 65, 74; *Il trionfo del Tempo e del Disingano,* 8, 14, 35; *Israel in Egypt,* 35, 40, 74; *Jephtha,* 36, 49, 74; *Joseph and His Brethren,* 46; *Joshua,* 74; *Judas Maccabaeus,* 50, 74; *La Resurrezione,* 8, 14, 15; *Messiah* (see separate entry); *Samson,* 42, 45, 46, 50, 74, 95; *Saul,* 35, 40, 46, 73; *Solomon,* 48, 50; *Theodora,* 73, 95; other: *Aci, Galatea e Polifemo,* 30; *Acis and Galatea,* 20, 29, 30-31, 35, 42; *Alexander's Feast,* 35, 42, 48; *Anthem on the Peace,* 48; *Brockes's Passion,* 11; cantatas (secular Italian), 15, 96, 100, 107, 113; Chandos Anthems, 20; Coronation anthems, 30, 135; *Dixit Dominus,* 14; *Foundling Hospital Anthem,* 48; *Haman and Mordechai,* 20, 29; *L'Allegro, il Penseroso ed il Moderato,* 35, 42; *Laudate pueri,* 14; "My Heart Is Inditing," 30; *Nisi Dominus,* 14; *Ode for Saint Cecilia's Day,* 35; *Royal Fireworks,* 48; *Saint John Passion* (spurious), 10; "Zadok the Priest," 30

Haydn, Franz Joseph, 53, 56-57

Haymarket. *See* King's Theatre in the Haymarket

Heidegger, John Jacob, 28

Henry, Matthew, 96, 133, 147-148

Hiller, Johann Adam, 53
Hilton, John: *The Dialogue of Job, God, Satan, Job's Wife, and the Messengers*, 11; *King Solomon and the Two Harlots*, 11
Historia (musical genre), 9, 102
Holdsworth, Edward, 42, 46, 77, 84, 131
Horace, 68
Huddersfield Choral Society, 54
Humphreys, Samuel, 74

In Guilty Night. See Purcell, Henry

Jennens, Charles, 38-40, 42, 46, 65, 71, 77-78, 84-85, 103, 109, 131, 133
Jephte. See Carissimi, Giacomo
Johnson, Samuel, 24, 27, 28, 38, 67
Jonson, Ben, 68-69

Keiser, Reinhard, 11, 12; work: *Der blutige und sterbende Jesus*, 10
Kidder, Richard, 76-77
Kimball, Roger, 70
King Solomon and the Two Harlots. See Hilton, John
King's Theatre in the Haymarket, 17, 18, 20, 21, 28-29, 30, 31, 32, 46, 53

Lampe, John-Frederick. *See Dragon of Wantley, The*
Larsen, Jens Peter, 65, 119, 120, 126, 127
Lauda (musical genre), 4
Lincoln's Inn Fields, 24
Linton, Michael, 118
Luckett, Richard, 31, 54

Madrigalism, 83-84
Mainwaring, John, 14, 15, 16
Marissen, Michael, 85, 133
Marsden, George, 131
Masque, 16, 20
Mattheson, Johann, 11, 12, 69, 71, 73

Messiah: borrowings, 96, 100, 107, 113, 124; and Handel's oratorios, similarities, 37; and Handel's oratorios, uniqueness, 37; musical genres in, 82-83; performance history of, 54-61; reception, Dublin, 42-44; reception, London, 44-46; reception, worldwide, 53-54; revisions, 95-96, 129
Milton, John, 35, 128
Morell, Thomas, 74
Mozart, Wolfgang Amadeus, 59

Neri, St. Philip, 4, 6
New Music Hall in Fishamble Street. *See* Dublin
Nichols, John, 39, 54

Opera: in England, 16-18; origin, 4, 6. *See also* Handel, George Frideric, works: operas, and opera, Italian in England
Opera of the Nobility, 31
Oratorio: criticism of, 10; definition, 3; forerunners, 4, 6-7; in England, 11; in Germany, 9-10; in Italy, 7-8; and opera, relation to, 4, 35-36; origin, 4
Ottoboni, Cardinal Pietro, 14

Pamphili, Cardinal Benedetto, 14
Peri, Jacopo: *Dafne*, 6; *Eurydice*, 6
Pope, Alexander, 25, 85
Purcell, Henry: *Dido and Aeneas*, 8, 17, 131; *In Guilty Night*, 11

Queen's Theatre in the Haymarket. *See* King's Theatre in the Haymarket

Rappresentatione di Anima, et di Corpo, 6
Restoration, 17
Rhetoric, musical, 83-84
Rich, John, 24-25

Index

Roubiliac, Louis François, 51
Royal Academy of Music, 21, 22, 28
Ruspoli, Marquis Francesco Maria, 14, 15

Scarlatti, Alessandro, 15
Scarlatti, Domenico, 15
Schütz, Heinrich, 9, 83
Senesino, 31
Shaw, George Bernard, 57-58, 60
Siege of Rhodes, The, 16
Smith, Ruth, 40, 74, 132
Smither, Howard, 9, 65, 67
Steevens, George, 38-39
Sydney, Sir Philip, 68, 70
Synge, Dr. Edward, 43-44, 71

Taruskin, Richard, 53, 72-73
Taylor, John, 50

Telemann, Georg Philipp, 11
Theatre Royal in Drury Lane, 17, 18
Three Choirs Festival, 49, 53
Tobin, John, 129

Van Til, Marian, 49
Vauxhall Gardens, 51
Venus and Adonis. See Blow, John
Vickers, Brian, 40
Virgil, 84-85

Watts, Isaac, 131
Westminster Abbey, 51, 56-57
Wyatt, Sir Thomas, 69

Yancey, Philip, 141-142

Zachau, Friedrich Wilhelm, 12